# CELTIC LEGENDS
## of
# PEMBROKESHIRE

Also published by Llanerch:

CELTIC LEGENDS OF GLAMORGAN
Anthony Rhys

TALIESIN POEMS
trans. Meirion Pennar

THE BLACK BOOK OF CARMARTHEN
trans. Meirion Pennar

SYMBOLISM OF THE CELTIC CROSS
Derek Bryce

THE CELTIC SOURCES OF THE
ARTHURIAN LEGEND
Jon Coe & Simon Young

BARDS AND HEROES:
an introduction to Old Welsh poetry
CARL LOFMARK

For a complete list of c.250 titles
write to LLANERCH PUBLISHERS
FELINFACH
LAMPETER
CEREDIGION
WALES
SA48 8PJ

All Llanerch books are printed in Wales.

# CELTIC LEGENDS
## of
# PEMBROKESHIRE

written and illustrated

by

ANTHONY RHYS

ISBN 1 86143 073 6

LLANERCH PUBLISHERS,
FELINFACH.

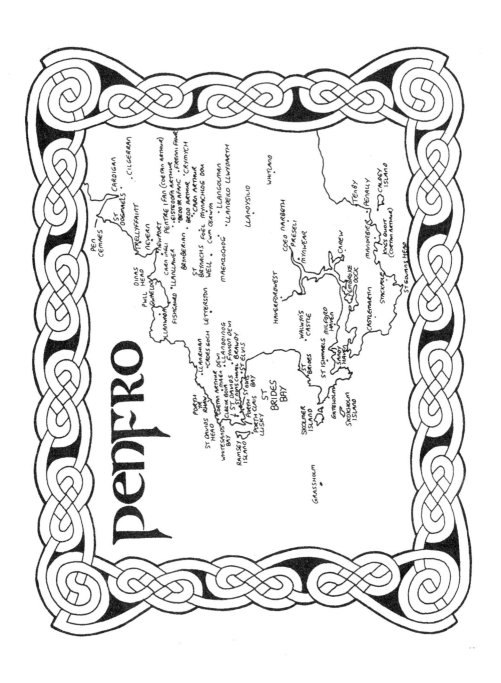

## Acknowledgements

I would like to thank the University of Wales Press for permission to publish poetry from the *'The Beginnings of Welsh Poetry: Studies by Ifor Williams'*. I also wish to thank the staff at Harrow library for obtaining many of the source books used in writing this book, especially Audrey and So-Mei. Michael Tibbetts and Eddie Marr also deserve recognition for proof reading the manuscript. The most thanks must go to Derek and John; without their help this book would never have been published.

Dedicated to Nanny

With fond memories of John

# Contents

Map of the Tales 2
Preface 6
Introduction 7
The Mabinogion Legends 14

Pwyll Lord of Dyfed 14
Pryderi 26
Manawydan Son of Llyr 39

The Age Of Saints 54

St David 58
St Teilo 74
St Govan 79
St Brynach 77
St Patrick & Ireland 76
Female Saints 80
Caldey Island 84
Gateholm Island 86
Holy Wells 87

The Legends 93

The Great Boar Hunt 93
Praising Tenby 101
King Arthur's Stones 103
Gwalchmai and Walwyn's
Castle 105
Giants 107
Beddau 109
Magic Stones 110
Hen Ci Bal 114
The Killer Toads of Cemais 115

The Tylwyth Teg 117

Rhys the Deep 117
The Otherworld 120
The Fountain of Knowledge 123
The Tragedy of Llech y Derwydd 127
Pergrin and the Mermaid 130
Ianto and the Fairy Money 133

Further Reading 135
Bibliography 137

# Preface

This book is a companion to Celtic Legends of Glamorgan also published by Llanerch. The illustrations in the book are by the author and are intended to bring some imagery to the tales.

# Introduction

The county of Pembrokeshire, which covers the south-west peninsula of Wales, has been called 'The Little England beyond Wales' but for me its beauty lies purely in its Welshness. From the cairn-covered hills of Preseli in the north to the tiny chapel of Saint Gofan in the south, Pembrokeshire is a county rich in tradition and legend. These traditions are not things that can exist independently by themselves. They cannot be removed and placed anywhere else in the world because their roots and origins dig deep into the soil of the fields, the rocks of the mountains and the waters of the coast. The land would only be a skeleton if you stripped away the flesh of its past and in this book I hope to show you that the beauty of Pembrokeshire lies as much in the breath of the storyteller as it does in green fields and blue waters.

The landscape, so often thought of as a dead entity to build and live upon, is alive with meanings and we read these meanings like a book. When we walk or drive through an area that we are familiar with we associate our lives with the places we see. Familiar streets, buildings and trees all work with our memories to create the feel of a place, either feelings of knowing and belonging or feelings of strangeness. In this way the stories in this book have been attached to the landscape for generations and have become an integral part of it. They are the legends of the Welsh people, the Cymry, who have lived on the peninsula of Pembrokeshire for over two thousand years. The stories of the hills, mountains, rivers, coasts, wells, churches and forts all play a part in bringing the culture, history and very soul of Pembrokeshire alive.

## A Brief Geography and History

Pembrokeshire has been a county since 1536 when the Act of Union forced Wales into the same administrative system as England. Many centuries previous to this the south-west peninsula of Wales was the ancient homeland of the Demetae, the Celtic tribe which existed before the Roman invasion. The Demetae gave their name to Dyfed although at that time the area would probably have consisted of many small kingdoms, loosely unified into a wider tribal unit. Traces of these ancient divisions have survived in the seven cantrefs of Dyfed namely Pebidiog, Cemais, Emlyn, Gwarthaf, Penfro, Daugleddau and Rhos. The cantref is a Welsh unit of land and the word literally means 'one hundred homesteads'. It was these same seven cantrefs that Pwyll Lord of Dyfed ruled over in an ancient legend.

In the early middle ages these cantrefi were halved to form commotes and they continued to be ruled by minor chieftains who were themselves ruled by the kings of Dyfed. The area was even later divided into the hundreds of Cemais, Dewsland, Cilgerran, Dungleddy, Narberth, Castlemartin and Roose. These divisions roughly followed the earlier boundaries of the cantrefs with the exception that Cantre Gwarthaf in the east became a large part of what is now Carmarthenshire. These hundreds are also now divided into many parishes and in the text where I mention a place name I have tried to place it in its broader parish or hundred for easy identification.

Pembrokeshire's main geographical feature is its long coastline, which is now mainly protected by the Pembrokeshire Coast National Park. The area is also roughly divided into the hilly north which holds the Preseli mountains and the flatter south. Its south-west coastal position meant that sea travel was the main transport and the area once enjoyed very close contacts with Ireland, Cornwall, Brittany and the rest of coastal western Europe as far as Spain. Pembrokeshire's position on the sea routes greatly influenced it history when Christianity came very early to this part of Wales during the age of the saints. The stories of saints like St David, St Brynach and St Teilo show the close cultural links that existed between all the countries on the western seaboard. Pembrokeshire was no cultural backwater in the dark ages and its religious centre of St Davids emerged as one of the main foundations of the Celtic Church.

Pembrokeshire's coastal position and its proximity to Ireland had another huge effect on its early history for during and after the Roman occupation large numbers of Irish settled in the area. They came mainly from the Waterford area on Ireland's south-east coast and settled Dyfed in waves spreading from the fourth to the early sixth century. The Deisi and the Ui Liathan tribe that once ruled Dyfed have left behind a large number of inscribed stones in the Irish Ogham script which give us the names of some of their kings.

These Irish kings ruled large area of Wales but over the centuries they were engulfed by the majority population and so became merged with the Welsh ruling families.

Although some Welsh kings of the dark ages were not too keen to celebrate the Irish origins of their royal lines most of the great royal houses of Dyfed were descendants of these early Irish settlers. Tryffin ap Rhain was the last ruler of the pure Irish dynasty but the line continued indirectly with Hyfaidd ap Bleiddig and Llywarch whose daughter married the great Hywel Dda. The native Welsh rulers for much of the dark and early middle ages ruled Pembrokeshire. This period would have seen the massive growth of Christianity in Britain and was a sort of golden age for native rule in Wales.

All this began to change however with the defeat and death in 1093 of Rhys ap Tewdwr. He was the ruler of Deheubarth, an area which covered most of south west Wales including Pembrokeshire, and with his death the Norman invasion began. In the following centuries Norman lordships were set up in many areas of Pembrokeshire and apart from the occasional rebellion and the victories of people like Rhys ap Gruffydd in the twelfth century the area came under Norman control.

Due to the Norman invasion Pembrokeshire became roughly divided into two sections of north and south. The invading Normans first heavily settled the better agricultural land of the south while the Welsh population was killed or driven to the hilly and mountainous regions of the north. Even after the Welsh ruling classes of the northern part of the county were defeated there was still the general division of an unmarked border between the cultures of the new population and the old. This cultural and language division survives today as generally speaking the county still has a more Welsh speaking north and an Anglicised south.

This historical divide has been mentioned because it has influenced the contents of this book. Although the legends and stories from the middle age manuscripts relate to the whole of Pembrokeshire when we look at the later folklore and place-name legends the north of the county, especially Dewsland, Cemais and Cilgerran, is infinitely richer than the south. This is because unfortunately the English south had much of its folklore and ancient place-names swept away quite early by the Flemish and Norman colonisation. Under this influence churches were rededicated to exclude the Welsh Celtic saints and ancient stones and burial chambers were also renamed and so for example 'Arthur's Stone' would have been renamed as 'Harold's Stone'. A quick look at the map at the beginning of the book will show however that the south of the county, although lacking in folklore, is still well represented in the manuscripts. The three Mabinogion stories are all set in Narbeth, there is the poem about ancient Tenby and there is the legend of the ancient chapel of St Govan's.

## Sources

The sources of the tales in this book are as wide and as diverse as the tales themselves. The oldest source used is the poem on Tenby, probably belonging to the ninth or tenth century which is in the medieval Book of Taliesin. The Mabinogion stories, the triads and saints' lives also come from other medieval Welsh manuscripts. Although these manuscripts date to the middle ages they all contain material which draws on much older traditions, material which can shed some light on the Welsh dark ages. Many of these sources, such as the lives of the saints, were written in Latin or Middle Welsh and they originated in the monastic foundations of Wales. We know the authors of some of these manuscripts, such as Rhigyfarch, a clergyman at Llanbadarn Fawr who wrote a 'Life of St David', but many of the manuscripts' writers, and also the places where they were written are unknown to us. It is fortunate indeed that we have a good selection of writings for this period as so many other manuscripts have not survived.

These old manuscripts are very important for our early material but for most of the later folklore and traditions we are indebted to the folklorists, antiquarians and gentlemen travellers of the last few centuries. The writings of figures like Richard Fenton who wrote a 'Historical Tour through Pembrokeshire' in 1811 and George Owen's 'Description of Pembrokeshire' written in 1603 are invaluable because they recorded many local traditions and folklore. During the last century and the beginning of this one, local writers, poets and academics realised that folklore was dying out and so went about recording as much as they could find. Many of their

10

collections were published as books or appeared in local newspapers and periodicals. These folklorists who scoured the country recorded all sorts of material from the people of Wales, many of whom were old and who would have died a few years later and taken all their traditions with them. Because of this valuable work much has been recorded for posterity and although we now only have a fraction of what once existed, enough has been saved to illustrate the rich traditions and heritage of Wales.

The practice of folklore collecting was carried on well into this century by others, especially Robin Gwyndaf of the Welsh Folk Museum, who has collected written and oral narratives from the people of Wales. All of this information, from the ancient manuscripts to the recent recordings, has been studied by academics and this has recently led to a blossoming of our knowledge of the traditions and characters of the Welsh legends. There is still very much research to be done but these critical studies have made a book like this possible and hopefully this book will do all the centuries of precious work a little justice.

Place-names are also a very valuable source of evidence as they reflect the culture of the land and many of them are probably as old as the dark ages. The names of churches and wells tell us much about the period of the early saints and likewise the names of other features give us a background to the other characters of an area. King Arthur, St David, monsters, fairies and giants are all common in place names and they serve in many cases to give a real physical locality to the stories and legends.

This book itself is divided into four different sections, the Mabinogion, the saints, the legends and the Tylwyth Teg. Included in each of these chapters is a selection of tales and legends as well as a discussion on their background and meaning. This gives a much wider perspective of the history and culture behind the stories and hopefully dispels the modern myth that legends and folklore were meant only to amuse children and 'simple peasant folk'. The stories do entertain but lying underneath their surface is important information about the social values and traditions of the Welsh people and these meanings can only be properly understood by looking closely at the Celtic culture which has survived in Wales for thousands of years.

# The Map

The map at the beginning of the book is there to help the reader pinpoint the places that are mentioned in the text. All the places that have a substantial legend or piece of folklore about them have been marked on this map as a guide to the reader. If you are travelling or live in the area I hope some of these places will be ones you are visiting or already know of. It is my main intention that this book tells the story of the land of Pembrokeshire, so if you are travelling around the area the best maps to use to find the places mentioned in the book are the 2 large OS 1:25000 Outdoor Leisure maps of Pembrokeshire (Nos. 35 & 36). These maps cover almost the entire county from the north coast to the south and are invaluable to any traveller.

PENN ANNWFN

# Chapter One

## The Mabinogion Legends

## Pwyll, Lord of Dyfed

The most famous Welsh legends must be those contained in the White Book of Rhydderch and the Red Book of Hergest that date from c.1325 and c.1400 AD respectively. The stories in these manuscripts are better known as the Mabinogion, the name their 19th century English translator gave them. She was Lady Charlotte Guest, a scholar and the wife of the ironmaster of Dowlais ironworks in Merthyr Tydfil. She called her translation the Mabinogion because in the manuscript four of the tales are described as branches of the 'Mabinogi' a term that may mean 'tales of youth'.

Each branch is a well-crafted medieval tale with roots in ancient Welsh mythology. Because the manuscripts seem to have been written in South Wales Pembrokeshire is very much the scene of many of the tales. There is the saga-like tale of Pwyll, his son Pryderi, their wives Rhiannon and Cigfa and their friend Manawydan. All this is set against the background of Pembrokeshire and the court at Arberth, now Narberth in south Pembrokeshire. The first branch of the Mabinogi introduces us to Pwyll Lord of Dyfed and his court at Arberth. Pwyll is a hero of legend rather than of history and his tale is told in three parts, each of them full of magic and wonder. In the first part of the legend, which is given here, he meets with Arawn the Lord of Annwn, the Welsh Otherworld. Pwyll's name translated from Welsh means 'wisdom, understanding' and in the beginning of his story we see these are qualities that Pwyll has not yet learned.

Pwyll was Lord over the seven cantrefs of Dyfed, that is the three cantrefs of Ystrad Tywi and the four of Ceredigion. His chief court was at Arberth, in the south of his domain and one day while he was resting there his thoughts turned to hunting. His horse and his finest hunting dogs were made ready and he set out for the forest of Glyn Cuch, which was the best hunting ground in all of Dyfed. As it was already late he only travelled as far as a place called Pen Llwyn

14

Diarwya. There he slept the night, and in the morning made himself
ready for the day's hunting.

Reaching Glyn Cuch he blew the hunting horn and let his dogs
off into the woods to seek out some prey. He tried to keep up with
the dogs but they moved swiftly through the thick forest and he
soon became separated from them. After searching for a while he
stopped to listen out for the dogs baying. From a distance he heard
the cry of a pack of dogs and spurred his horse towards them. The
cries sounded strange to him and they moved so quickly that he
twisted this way and that through the forest for what seemed like an
age. He thought he would never find them but soon enough he
burst out of the forest into the open air.

In front of him on the other side of the clearing he saw a strange
pack of dogs. They were chasing a large stag and as Pwyll looked
on the dogs swiftly brought the exhausted animal to the ground. As
they did so Pwyll wondered at the marvellous colour of the dogs.
Their bodies were of the purest white, unblemished apart from
bright blood-red ears and while he stood there in amazement his
own pack burst out of the forest from behind him. Without a
second thought he drove off the strange dogs and set his pack onto
the fallen stag, claiming the animal as his own.

A rider dressed in fine grey and brown hunting garments
approached Pwyll. He rode a dapple-grey horse and the strange
white dogs followed close behind him.

"Greetings to you!" Pwyll said to the new arrival.

"I know well enough who you are but I will not greet you," the
stranger said sternly.

"Is it your rank that stops you from greeting me?" asked Pwyll.

"I have enough rank to converse with you Pwyll but I choose not
to," he replied.

"Why then will you not greet me?" asked Pwyll, puzzled by the
stranger's behaviour.

"Because of your rudeness! My own pack took down that stag
yet you claim it for your own. You deserve dishonour from me to
the value of a hundred stags and you certainly do not deserve to be
greeted as a friend."

"I apologise for the dishonour I have done to you and I will make
it up to you according to your rank."

"In my own land I am a crowned king as you are," said the

15

stranger.

"And of what land are you king?" asked Pwyll.

"I am Arawn, King of Annwn," he replied.

"How may I repay you then King Arawn? It is my duty to heed your request."

"There is one thing you can do for me," explained Arawn, "a king whose realm borders onto my own has caused me problems in all my years of rule. He has harassed and attacked me constantly, so often that my lands have never known peace. Hafgan King of Annwn is his name and you can earn my friendship and trust by defeating him for me," explained Arawn.

"I will gladly do that if a bond of friendship can be made between us, but tell me how this can be accomplished," said Pwyll.

"That is easy enough. We shall become friends now and I will put a spell on you so that you will take on my appearance. When you are so disguised no-one will recognise you as any man other than myself. Then you will go to my fine court where you will live among my people for a year. There you will have the best of servants, the tastiest food and my beautiful wife to comfort you every night. When your task has been accomplished and Hafgan is dead we shall meet back here, a year and a day from now."

"How will I know which man is Hafgan?" asked Pwyll.

"That is also easy. We have arranged to meet and fight a year from today at a ford on the border of our realms. You will fight him there in front of my nobles for the right to rule Annwn. There is one word of advice I must give you and that is this; you must strike him only once with a well-aimed and crushing blow. He will beg you to strike him again a second time and a third time but you must not. When we fought together before no matter how many times I struck him he would always be alive ready to engage me the next day."

"I will gladly do what you have asked," agreed Pwyll, "but what will become of my own kingdom while I am gone?"

"That is another easy question to answer. I will take your shape and watch over your lands while you rule over mine," said Arawn, "Come, follow me now. We must go to my realm."

Pwyll followed Arawn across a land that he did not recognise to a handsome court. It was the finest sight he had ever seen.

"This is my land and that is my court," said Arawn, "They are now yours for a year. Enter the court and you will be greeted as myself and made welcome," said Arawn and then he left.

Pwyll entered the court and there he saw rich dwellings and marble buildings which gleamed all around him. As he dismounted his horse he was immediately waited upon by servants who took his hunting clothes from him and replaced them with a rich cloak made from gold brocade. His boots were taken from him and his horse was led away to rest as he sat down and watched the servants preparing for a feast.

Troops of men began to enter the hall and take their seats. Pwyll wondered at them for never before had he seen so many brave, well-dressed warriors all together in the same place. A beautiful woman also entered and everyone greeted her as their queen. She was dressed in shining golden garments and was attended by handmaids, each of whom was as lovely as the best woman in his own land. Pwyll immediately felt a great fondness for her, as she was the most beautiful woman he had ever set eyes upon.

After everyone had washed they sat down, Pwyll at the head of the table with the queen to one side and the earl to the other. Golden jewelled plates and bowls were brought in and they were full of the most delicious food Pwyll had ever tasted. All through the night there was a great celebration that rang with laughter and Pwyll enjoyed himself more than he had ever done before. He conversed with the queen and soon found her to be the sweetest and kindest woman he had ever met.

When it was time to sleep all the court bade Pwyll farewell and the queen went with him to a comfortable chamber. Pwyll had been talking fondly all night with the queen but when they entered the chamber he went straight to bed and turned to face away from her. Not one word or touch came from Pwyll until the morning when they rose from the chamber. From then on, even though they were courteous and affectionate to each other by day when they went to bed Pwyll would turn over and go straight to sleep. For the whole year not a word was spoken or a touch exchanged between them during the night.

Pwyll spent many days at the court, hunting, singing, dancing and feasting. He had never had a more enjoyable time. When the year was over all the nobles from the realm assembled together and prepared themselves to meet Hafgan and his army on the ford. That

17

morning Pwyll armed himself and set out with his men. Hafgan had already reached the ford and was waiting there with his nobles on the other side of the river. One of Arawn's knights stepped forward to make a proclamation.

"All those present here know of the battle between these two kings over the right to rule this land," he said. "The fight will be resolved in single combat at this ford and their own strength shall be the test of their right to rule."

Pwyll rode out and met Hafgan at the ford. The two kings faced each other across the river and then charged. They met in the middle of the river and clashed furiously. Pwyll hit Hafgan with a tremendous blow that split his shield in two, the force sending him over the back of his horse. He landed on the bank of the river with his armour cracked and his body fatally wounded.

"What right did you have to strike me, for I have done you no injury!" said Hafgan, who knew, because of his magic, that he was not facing Arawn himself.

"Now that you have won finish me off! Strike me again!" begged Hafgan.

"I have struck you enough," said Pwyll. "If anyone else here has quarrel enough to strike you let them do so but I will not touch you again."

"Then take me away from here so that I may die in peace!" shouted Hafgan to one of his nobles knowing that he was defeated and he was taken away.

"Who among you will join with me now?" Pwyll asked the host, "Who would you have rule Annwn now?"

The assembled nobles talked amongst themselves and agreed that the man who they thought was Arawn should rule over Annwn.

"We should all be your men now for you are the victor and Annwn is now yours by right because of it," replied one of the men.

"Then let all here swear submission to me, as is my right, and those who will not let them be compelled to do so by my sword," demanded Pwyll.

All the nobles that were assembled at the ford swore loyalty to Pwyll and gave their allegiance to him. By the next day the two halves of the country were united under Pwyll and Annwn was one country.

Pwyll then rode out to Glyn Cuch to meet Arawn as had been

arranged.

"Greetings friend" said Pwyll, "How fares Dyfed since I have been gone?"

"Your land prospers more than ever. Now your debt to me is paid I am glad to see a friend before me," replied Arawn.

The two greeted each other heartily and Pwyll's own shape was soon restored to him. Then after the two had talked for a while they returned to their own lands.

Arawn entered his court happy to be among his friends after such a long absence. He greeted them with so much happiness that everyone thought he was acting mad. Although he had really been gone a year they all thought they had seen him just that morning. Nevertheless he declared a feast to be held and that night there was much dancing and singing until it was time to go to bed. When Arawn and the queen went to bed Arawn kissed and caressed her as he had always done.

"Why, after all this time, have you chosen tonight to touch and converse with me?" asked the queen after they had finished their lovemaking.

"Do we not always love each other so when we are together?" asked Arawn puzzled.

"For the last year you have not spoken a word to me or touched me in this bed," explained the queen. "All you have done is turn your back to me and sleep."

"What a faithful friend I have found! I am happy to have met Pwyll," exclaimed Arawn. "Do not be angry with me, wife, for it was not me sharing this bed with you this past year," and so Arawn told his queen all that had happened.

"That is indeed a good friend that you have found, for him to have refused the temptations of the flesh for so long," said his wife.

"They were my thoughts as well," said Arawn.

Meanwhile Pwyll had arrived back at his court and was filled with joy when he saw his people and his home again. After he had dismounted he asked his nobles how well he had ruled in the last year.

"You have never ruled so wisely, with such generosity and kindness as you have in the past year, lord," they answered.

Pwyll was pleased that he had met Arawn and he explained to everyone what had happened.

"That is a good friend you have found," they said, "will the good rule that we have enjoyed still continue, lord?"

"If I am able to continue it I will do so," said Pwyll

From then on a great friendship was made between the two rulers and they met often. They sent each other gifts of horses, dogs and hawks whenever they fancied and their two lands became great allies. Because of Pwyll's stay in Annwn and his fight with Hafgan he was called 'Lord of Dyfed' less and less until eventually the title of 'Pwyll Head of Annwn' took its place."

In this tale we see how Annwn, the Welsh Otherworld, is a beautiful place filled with the best of all things. More importantly though, we see how dependent this 'wondrous land' was on our own imperfect world. The Celtic Otherworld was not an untouchable heaven and the main theme in this story is of an Otherworld king who asks a mortal for help. This found in other Celtic legends and in an Irish tale the hero Cu Chulainn is offered an Otherworld woman if he will help the Otherworld king, Labraid the Swift Sword-Wielder, fight against his enemies in Mag Mell, 'The Plain of Delight'. The Welsh Annwn and the Irish Mag Mell were full of different Otherworld tribes fighting each other for supremacy and so were just like the mortal lands.

Arawn and Hafgan are locked in an eternal fight and Arawn must have been magically bound to always give Hafgan a second blow and revive him ready to fight again the next day. Pwyll, on the other hand, being a mortal and a stranger was able to hit Hafgan once and kill him, breaking the cycle of never-ending struggle between the two lords and winning the magical battle for Arawn.

This endless battle between Arawn and Hafgan for the rulership of Annwn may also have a deeper symbolic meaning. One scholar has suggested that Arawn's grey-brown clothing and Hafgan's name, which may mean 'summer-white', points to a symbolic summer-winter battle between the two. The two kings would then be fighting the endless seasonal battle for control over the land during the spring and autumn. There is a similar legend mentioned elsewhere in the Mabinogion where Gwyn and Gwthur fight for the love of the maiden Creudylad every May-day. Gwyn is also a lord of the Welsh Otherworld and Gwthur's full name means 'Victor son of Light'. The tale is about winter fighting summer for control of

20

spring, which is represented by the woman. This structure may lie behind the story of Annwn and Hafgan, although Pwyll in defeating Hafgan, who represents summer, must have brought about winter, which is a strange symbolic thing for an up and coming young hero to do.

The fact that Pwyll doesn't find a wife during his stay in the Otherworld is also rather strange. In Celtic tradition the mortal hero usually found a magical partner on their Otherworld quest. In the Irish story mentioned above Cu Chulainn, while in the Otherworld, wins the love of a fairy woman called Fann, the daughter of a god, and ends up sleeping with her. Pwyll does no such thing and shows self-restraint when he sleeps with Arawn's wife. Here the point is not to show how he gains a wife in the Otherworld but how he displays his virtue and self-control. This later medieval adaptation of the story means however that the storyteller still has to explain how Pwyll gained his wife.

In the second part of the story Pwyll does find his Otherworld wife. He meets her while he sits on Gorsedd Arberth, 'The Mound of Arbeth', a magical hill which, when sat upon by someone of royal blood, would either cause them harm or show them a wonder. Pwyll is not harmed and he sees the wonderful Rhiannon riding past. This future queen of Dyfed is in fact a Celtic goddess and the name Rhiannon is related to 'Rigantona' meaning 'Great Queen'. She is therefore an ancient horse goddess similar to the Gaulish Epona or the Irish Macha.

When Pwyll actually meets with Rhiannon he finds that he has another quest to overcome. She loves Pwyll but has been promised by her father to another man called Gwawl. A feast for Pwyll is held at Rhiannon's court and during the feast a stranger enters and asks Pwyll for a gift. Pwyll promises that he will give him anything in his power but the stranger turns out to be Gwawl and he takes Rhiannon as his promised gift. Before Rhiannon is taken away however she tells Pwyll how he can win her back. Exactly a year later Pwyll follows her advice and manages to trick Gwawl, trapping him in Rhiannon's magic bag of plenty, a symbol of the goddesses fertility. Pwyll and Rhiannon are then free to rule Dyfed together.

Rhiannon's part in the story is not merely that of a mortal wife. She is magically associated with horses in the story on three occasions. When Pwyll first sees Rhiannon she is riding a magic horse and, although she seems to be only trotting, he cannot catch her even on his fastest horse. When she is accused of her son's death, which will be told in the next chapter, her punishment is to stand at the horse mounting block. From here she has to carry guests into the court and so takes on the role of a horse. Also her missing son soon appears far away in a barn at the same time as a colt is born.

Rhiannon's role as Pwyll's wife and her association with horses becomes very clear when we look at the Celtic theme of the 'goddess of sovereignty'. This goddess symbolised the very land itself and was represented by the horse. It was of great importance in Celtic society for a human king to be symbolically linked with the land he ruled. It was the king's job to ensure that his land remained productive for his people and so in effect he had to 'marry' with the land to ensure its fertility.

Rhiannon is in effect the Welsh goddess of land and sovereignty. In the Irish version of this tale the goddess Macha also marries a rash mortal called Crunncha. His foolish boasts to the king of Ireland end with Macha being forced to race against the king's horses and even though she is nine months pregnant the king will not excuse her. She wins the horse race, which is not suprising as she is the goddess of horses, and immediately gives birth to twins. In her rage at being disrespected by the king of the land she curses all his men to feel terrible birth pains every time their land is in danger and this later leads to their homeland being ransacked.

This goddess was a very powerful symbol and her importance goes back to the pre-Roman Celts. There is even evidence of Celtic kings symbolically and physically mating with horses or bathing in a broth made from their flesh in order to achieve the symbolic union between king and land. In Pwyll's tale though he just has to marry Rhiannon in order to become an effective king, and with this point we come to the main meaning of the whole story of Pwyll.

Pwyll is tested throughout the tale and he has to learn to acquire the leadership skills of bravery, wisdom and self control. Through the taking of Arawn's stag he shows arrogance and pride in thinking that there is no other hunter greater than himself, or no other lord higher than himself. He then has to show his bravery, courage and restraint in the fight with Hafgan, for these three properties were

22

highly praised amongst Celtic kings. In Arawn's bed he also shows the quality of trustworthiness that bonds the friendship between the two rulers. The third and final test for Pwyll is to gain the hand of Rhiannon. He is foolish to begin with but soon he listens to Rhiannon's advice and overcomes Gwawl. In this, the most important lesson has been learnt and he can marry her and so become united with the goddess of the land.

The importance of a story like this becomes apparent when you consider that it would have been told to the young princes of the Welsh courts. When the story was written the English were pressing on the borders of Wales and the Welsh kings were also constantly fighting petty battles amongst themselves. A lesson of how to rule with strength and, more importantly, with wisdom and judgement was one that needed to be learnt. The tale of Pwyll, whose name meant 'reason, wisdom' was literally a tale of wisdom and reason for these future rulers of Wales to follow. Pwyll is also unknown in other Welsh tradition so his character and this version of an ancient Celtic tale was probably written with this purpose in mind.

As well as the moral background the legend is also full of magic and Celtic imagery. Arawn's white dogs are Otherwordly animals and they appear frequently in Celtic legend to either test or guide the hero in the Otherworld. In the third of the Mabinogi branches Manawydan and Pryderi are out hunting when they see a shining white boar that leads them to an Otherworld castle. Likewise King Arthur hunts a magic white hart in the tale of Gereint and Enid and the goddess Morrigan also fights with the hero Cu Chulainn in the guise of a white, red-eared cow. The whiteness of the animals and especially their red tipped ears was the sign that they had an Otherwordly origin and were faster, stronger and quicker-witted than their earthly counterparts.

The Mound of Arberth where Pwyll saw Rhiannon for the first time is one of the magical fairy mounds common in Celtic myth as gateways from one world to the other. It was said to be near his court at Arberth, which means it must be near the modern town of Narberth. The tradition that when people sat or slept at certain magic places they would either be injured or see a wonder is found all over Wales. An example is the grave of Taliesin in Ceredigion which, if slept upon for one night, would turn you into a madman or a poet. The same is said about the mountain of Cader Idris in north Wales and many megalithic sites such as Tinkinswood burial chamber in Glamorgan. Pwyll also meets Arawn while out in the forest of Glyn Cuch, part of the ancient cantref of Emlyn which is now in Cilgerran, and dense forests were also another gateway to the Otherworld.

To return to the Mabinogi story of Pwyll we read that after Pwyll and Rhiannon ruled together for three years the men of Dyfed began to worry that they would not produce a child. They called a meeting at Preseli, then the name of a place rather than the whole mountain area, and Pwyll asked for one more year to try and have a child, which they gladly granted him. At the end of this year a son was born to the couple and the tale of that son Pryderi will be told in the next chapter.

As to what happened to Pwyll Head of Annwn after his son was born, all we are told in the Mabinogi is this:

"And thus passed years and years, until the end of Pwyll the Chief of Annwn's life came, and he died."

Presumably his death was a peaceful one after all his lessons had been learnt and he ruled over Dyfed wisely. After his death the Lordship of Dyfed passed onto his son Pryderi and it is to his tale that we turn now.

# Pryderi

Pryderi the son of Pwyll, although he doesn't have a Mabinogi branch all to himself, is included in each of them; from his birth in the first branch to his death in the fourth branch. Pryderi ap Pwyll has good parentage for a Celtic hero, his father being the king Pwyll and his mother the Celtic goddess Rhiannon. With parents like these it is hardly surprising that his birth is not a simple affair but an event full of magic and the workings of the gods. The birth story itself comes from the Mabinogi branch of Pwyll, and so we need to go back to Arberth and also back in time a little, to when Pwyll and Rhiannon are expecting their child. Although the tale at times does seem a little muddled it is still a legend worthy of a hero.

After Rhiannon had given birth to Pryderi at Arberth she fell asleep exhausted, leaving the child in the care of her handmaids. Soon enough, however, the women fell asleep, even though they were meant to have been watching the mother and child carefully. When they awake at dawn the child had gone.

"The child is lost and so are we!" they lamented.

"Our punishment will be death for falling asleep and losing him," one woman cried. "Is there any hope for us?"

"There is hope for I have a plan," said one woman, "there is a deerhound in the court who has just had pups, we should kill some of them and leave their bones lying around. If we also put blood on Rhiannon's face it will look like she killed her child in a fit of madness. It will be her word against ours." The poor women were desperate and, not knowing what else to do, they settled on this plan.

Rhiannon woke as morning came and looked for her child but all she could see was blood and bones.

"Women, what has happened to my child?" she asked the maids in a panic.

"My lady we are bruised and beaten from struggling with you all night," the women answered. "You killed the child for you had the strength of one gripped with madness."

"Everyone here and the Lord God himself knows that not to be true," Rhiannon said, "do not be afraid, just tell me the truth."

"We will not let any harm come to us lady, what we speak is the truth," replied the women and no matter how hard she pleaded with them they would not change their story.

Pwyll Head of Annwn rose that day with his retinue and the news of what happened soon spread across the land. The nobles told Pwyll that he must leave his wife because of the terrible crime she had committed but Pwyll loved her and believed that she was innocent.

"You have no right to ask us to separate," Pwyll told his nobles, "a child is what you asked for and she has borne one, let the elders and the wise men decide on her punishment but I will not leave her."

So the wise men and elders were summoned and gave their judgement. Rhiannon was so weary of arguing with the women that she grudgingly accepted their counsel. Her punishment was to stand at the mounting block in the court of Arberth and tell her story to everyone who arrived at the court. She also had to offer to carry the visitors on her back into the court but thankfully it was only rarely that anyone accepted her offer for everyone knew she was a noble woman and a queen.

A year later in Gwent, at a place called Gwent-ys-Coed there lived a man named Teyrnon. He was the best man in the world and he also had one of the best horses in the world. This horse used to foal every May-Eve but before anyone could see the colt it would disappear without a trace. That May-Eve he was determined not to let this strange thing happen again and so he brought the horse inside and sat up to watch it throughout the night. As soon as night fell the horse gave birth to the sturdiest and strongest colt that Teyrnon had ever seen. He rose from his seat to examine the colt but as he did so a huge claw entered the window and grabbed the colt by its mane. Teyrnon drew his sword and hacked at the hideous claw. He managed to chop the monster's arm off at the elbow, leaving the colt safely inside the barn.

There was a terrible scream as the arm fell to the floor and so he quickly ran outside, determined to fight with the rest of the monster but that night it was so dark that he could see nothing. He considered chasing after the monster but decided to go back to see the colt instead. Inside the barn he was astonished to find a handsome baby lying next to the newly born colt and they were the two handsomest things he had ever seen.

27

He picked up the lad, who was already a heavy and strong baby and went to see his wife. She was sleeping so he woke her and handed her the child.

"A child is the only thing you have not had from me my love, and that is what I give you now," said Teyrnon.

"What is the story behind this!" she said in amazement and Teyrnon told her the tale, which only increased her amazement.

"Look at the cloth he is wrapped in!" she said. "It is fine silk, this child is of a noble birth."

"Are we not nobles ourselves?" remarked Teyrnon, and without knowing what else to do they decided to keep the child as their own.

The child was a great joy and comfort to them both. He was baptised in the customs of the time and was given the name Gwri Golden Hair for his hair was as yellow and as bright as the rays of the sun. The child grew up quickly. After he had only been with them for a year he could walk and had grown as big as a three year old. When he had been with them for two years he was as strong as a six year old and by the time he was four he was asking the stableboys if he could attend to the horses.

Teyrnon's wife saw this and asked her husband where the horse that was born on the same day as the child was kept now. ) —— now kept

"Why, he is in the stable being looked after," answered Teyrnon.

"Would it not be a good idea to give that horse to the boy as they were both found together on the same night," she said.

"That is a fine idea," said Teyrnon and he asked the stable boys to break the colt in ready for the time when the boy could ride it and achieve great deeds.

Eventually they heard the news about what had befallen Rhiannon, and Teyrnon listened intently to the stories. Those who had been to Arberth lamented greatly at Rhiannon's misfortune. Thinking about these sad stories he began to look closer at the boy. He had once been in Pwyll's attendance and by now the boy had grown so much that Teyrnon could not fail to see the striking resemblance between the lad and Pwyll.

Teyrnon was filled with worry and that night when he was alone with his wife he told her all that he had heard.

"It is not right to keep the boy any longer and let Rhiannon suffer more dishonour," he said.

His wife agreed with him, and they decided to take Gwri back to

28

Pwyll and Rhiannon.

"Although I am saddened by this we will gain in three ways," said Teyrnon's wife. "We will be thanked for releasing Rhiannon, we will have Pwyll's thanks for returning his son and we will have the boy's thanks when he grows into a man. He will be our foster son and he will look after us."

So the next day they set out for Arberth, with the boy riding his colt alongside them. When they reached the court they saw Rhiannon at the mounting block.

"Walk no further chieftain," she said, "for I will carry all of you into the court from here, it is my punishment for killing my child with my own hands."

"I do not think any of us here will allow you to carry us," answered Teyrnon and so they entered the court on foot.

Here they were welcomed heartily and, as Pwyll had just returned from a circuit of his lands, a feast was about to begin. They washed and sat themselves down to eat, Teyrnon sitting next to Pwyll and Rhiannon and the boy sitting behind them with Teyrnon's companions from Gwent-ys-Coed.

"I am glad to see you after so long," Pwyll said to Teyrnon.

"And I am glad to be here again," Teyrnon replied, and after the meal was completed Teyrnon stood and told the court the tale of how he had found the boy in his barn. He told of how he and his wife had brought the child up the last few years. Then he turned to Rhiannon.

"Look upon your son now Rhiannon, for you were wronged and have been the subject of many lies," said Teyrnon. "When I heard of your suffering I was so saddened that I came straight away and there will be no-one in this court who would deny that this is the son of Pwyll and yourself."

"If this is true, what a relief it is from my long anxiety!" exclaimed Rhiannon.

"You have named your son well!" said Pendaran Dyfed the Chieftain of Dyfed, "Let him be called Pryderi son of Pwyll, for that is surely the name that suits him best now that he has been found."

"What if his own name suits him better?" said Rhiannon. "What is the boy's name?"

"Gwri Golden-hair," replied Teyrnon and with this Pwyll stood up and addressed the court.

"I think it is right that he should be named according to the first words his mother uttered when she heard the good news about him." said Pwyll, and so the child was called Pryderi, or 'Anxiety', from then on.

"God thank you Teyrnon for bringing him back to us," said Pwyll, "when he grows into a man he should reward you well."

"My lord, it is my wife who will suffer from this, having brought up the child as her own for all this time, no one grieves more than she does over losing him." said Teyrnon.

"By my faith," said Pwyll, "you will be maintained by me as long as I am alive and able to do so, and if Pryderi lives he shall support you after that. If you and these nobles assembled here agree we will send him to be fostered now by Pendaran Dyfed and you shall all be companions and foster fathers to him."

This was agreed upon and the boy was given to the Chieftain of Dyfed and all the nobles swore alliance with him. Pryderi offered Teyrnon the finest jewels, horses and dogs as he left the court but he would not accept anything.

Pryderi remained in Dyfed and grew into a strong and handsome lad, the most skilled at feats in the whole country. After his father died he became lord of the seven cantrefs of Dyfed himself, ruling wisely and justly. He took over the three cantrefs of Ystrad Tywi and the four cantrefs of Ceredigion which are now called together the seven cantrefs of Seisyllwch. When he had finished campaigning and increasing his domains he took a wife and she was Cigfa daughter of Gwynn the Splendid son of Gloyw Wide Hair son of Casnar, one of the noblest men of this island."

All of the renowned Welsh heroes would have once had stories like this told about their wondrous birth but Pryderi's is the only one that has survived. The tale of the hero's birth set the scene for the events of the rest of his life but the story as we have it today seems to leave out a few important things. Who takes Pryderi in the first place and what is the mysterious claw that leaves him in Teyrnon's stable? Also there is the question of why the identity of his parents seems to constantly change and why he has so many father figures.

I mentioned in the last chapter that in an earlier version Pwyll should have gained a wife during his stay in Arawn's Otherworld court. If he had a child there and Arawn's wife turned out to be

Rhiannon then it could easily have been Arawn who stole the child in anger. Another possibility could be that because it takes Pwyll and Rhiannon three years to have a baby Pwyll himself is infertile. Then the possibility could be that Rhiannon had the child by a man from the Otherworld who later comes back to steal the child from her.

The problem of parentage gets even more confusing when Teyrnon and his wife bring up the child. They are also an infertile couple as Teyrnon says to his wife that he will give her the child, something which he could never give to her before. One interesting possibility arises from the introduction of Teyrnon because his name is related to 'Tigernonos' which means 'Great King'. We have already seen that Rhiannon was the 'Great Queen' who symbolised the fertility of the land and so Teyrnon and Rhiannon seem well matched. Pryderi would then be similar to 'Mabon' the divine son of the great king and queen in Celtic mythology.

What about Pendaren Dyfed, 'The Chieftain of Dyfed', who becomes Pryderi's foster father after he is returned to Rhiannon? He also becomes a candidate for Pryderi's father because in another source he is named as the original owner of Pryderi's magic Otherworld pigs. Arawn and Pwyll exchange gifts after they become friends and if the pigs were one of those gifts then the possibility arises that Pendaren Dyfed is another name for Arawn himself. If Pwyll was married to Rhiannon before he met Arawn then when the men swapped roles and beds Arawn/Pendaren could have slept with Rhiannon and would then be Pryderi's father.

As you can see, the question of Pryderi's parentage is a complicated one. It would seem a little less complicated however if we considered the role of fostering in Celtic society where a child was sent away to be brought up by other parents until he reached the age of manhood. It was considered improper for a father to be seen with his natural child before he reached manhood and the practice of fostering bound groups and tribes together in mutual alliances. Fostering, among the upper classes, was also known in Pembrokeshire as late as the eighteenth century. As Teyrnon and Pendaren Dyfed both appear in the role of foster-fathers maybe Teyrnon represents his Otherworld foster-father and Pendaren Dyfed his mortal foster-father.

The whole story is a puzzle but it is very likely that Pryderi's

31

parentage was a lot more complicated than just Pwyll and Rhiannon. Pwyll seems to take a back seat in the whole proceedings and he does not even see the child until it is brought to him many years later. Teyrnon and his mare are more important and as Rhiannon is a horse goddess this detail seems very important. Perhaps we are not dealing with simple questions of biological parents here but with a complex interplay of mythological motifs. Both Rhiannon and Teyrnon's mare have offspring which disappear when they are born and as Rhiannon is the horse goddess maybe she has to play the role of both horse and woman, giving birth to both the child and the colt who both then disappear.

The two men in all of this, Pwyll and Teyrnon, both appear as sterile guardians of mares after Rhiannon gives birth. Pwyll has to guard Rhiannon who, after her punishment, is a human doing the work of a horse and Teyrnon on that night guards a real horse who gives birth to a child. By stopping the claw from taking the newborn colt from the barn he prevents the mysterious force switching the boy and putting the colt in Pryderi's empty cot. It is significant that the colt is also given to Pryderi to ride when he returns to Rhiannon. In this her human and animal children are both united and now return to their human/animal mother. There are many possible explanations for the significance of Pryderi's birth but this mythological one explains many of the horse associations and Rhiannon's role in the story. No explanation properly reveals the owner of the mysterious claw however.

Pryderi's childhood after this is thankfully less problematic. His divine or hero status is shown in the speed at which he grows. By the time he is two he has the strength of a six year old and he proudly rides his colt to Arberth when he is only four years of age. This rapid growth is also seen in Irish myths. Another similarity with Pwyll can be found in the story of the most famous Irish hero Cu Chulainn. In his youth Cu Chulainn defeats a massive hound, and for this he is given the name of the 'Hound of Cu' as well as a taboo against eating dog's flesh. Pryderi also gains his name of 'anxiety' in childhood, losing his original name of Gwri, and it is possible that he would have had a similar taboo against horse flesh, especially because his mother is a mythical personification of the horse. The Pryderi/horse and Cu Chulainn/hound link could also be

32

explained as some sort of totem animal link, where each hero had a special relationship with the strengths of their respective animal protectors.

The wife that Pryderi takes at the end of the story is, like his mother Rhiannon, not a mortal woman. She is named as Cigva daughter of Gwynn the Splendid son of Gloyw Wide Hair. This Gwynn is the Lord of the Otherworld and King of the Fairies in medieval Welsh tradition. His father Gloyw Wide Hair or 'Shining Wide Hair' must also be a now forgotten god. The name of Gloyw Gwalltir, 'Shining Long Hair', also appears as the mythical ancestor of the great king Vortigern in an ancient genealogy. The name Cigva in the Irish language is Ciocba and she was the wife of one of the sons of Partholon, one of the first mythical settlers of Ireland. If there once existed a lost story about how Pwyll and Cigfa got together it is now unfortunately lost and nothing but these tantalising associations remain.

Pryderi's next appearance after his birth is in 'Branwen Daughter Of Llyr', the second branch of the Mabinogi. In this branch Bran, a god of immense stature who rules over all the Island of Britain, goes on an expedition to Ireland to retrieve his daughter Branwen who is being mistreated there by her husband King Mallolwch. The two kings fight and the battle turns into a great slaughter because the Irish have a cauldron of rebirth that they use to bring their dead warriors back to life. Eventually this cauldron is destroyed but only seven men escape from the carnage. Bran however has been fatally wounded in the battle. As he cannot walk back to Wales and his body is too large for him to be carried he asks the seven men to decapitate him. The warriors do this and Pryderi is among the seven who take Bran's magical severed head back to Britain.

Bran, who can still speak with the warriors, tells them to take his head and bury it in London as a talisman to protect the Island of Britain. During the journey however the seven warriors spend eighty years resting on an island called Gwales. This island is probably Grassholm off Pembrokeshire's west coast. Here on this Otherworld isle they live in luxury in a royal court and forget all of their sorrow spending the eighty years feasting in untroubled bliss. These eighty years were called 'The Feast of the Wondrous Head' and the feasting lasted until one of them opened a door they were told to keep shut. This action lets all the sorrow and pain back into their hearts and they must then return to the normal world.

Otherworld isles like Gwales were places of recuperation in Celtic myth. The most famous example of this is when King Arthur went to Avalon, an Otherworld isle, after he was badly wounded in a battle. The islands off the west coast of the Celtic lands were the most magical and so the islands off the Pembrokeshire coast such as Grassholm were once sacred. They were considered to be the magical lands where the Otherworld gods lived, and in many cases where people went when they died. We will come back to this aspect of Celtic myth in the chapter on the Tylwyth Teg where these fairy isles appear in stories that were still told this century.

The third branch of the Mabinogi, 'Manawydan Son of Llyr' leads directly on from the second branch. Although Pryderi appears briefly in it as a prisoner the main character is Manawydan and so I have left this story for the next chapter.

In the story of Pryderi's life his part in 'Math Son of Mathonwy', the last branch of the Mabinogion, is more important. Math is the Lord of Gwynedd and the legend says that he cannot live unless his feet are kept in a virgin's lap. The problem is that Gilfaethwy, his nephew, falls in love with this virgin, the footholder Goewin. He becomes sick with his love for she cannot be separated from Math. Gwydion, Gilfaethwy's brother, sees his love for Goewin and formulates a plan to help, knowing that Math can only leave his footholder in times of war:

Gwydion and Gilfaethwy went to see Math at his court in Gwynedd to tell him they had important news.

"Lord," said Gwydion, "I have heard of some strange creatures that have arrived in the south, creatures that have never been seen before on the whole island."

"What are these creatures called?" asked Math.

"They are known as pigs, lord," replied Gwydion.

"And what are the properties of these creatures?"

"They are small animals but their flesh is better than oxen or sheep," said Gwydion.

"Where are these creatures now?" asked Math.

"They are with Pryderi son of Pwyll in the south, lord. They were given to him by Arawn Lord of Annwn in a bond of friendship," explained Gwydion.

"How to you propose to get them for me Gwydion, since that is what you must be planning," said Math.

"You are right my lord, I intend to be received in Pryderi's court as one of a party of twelve bards and we will request them from him."

"He will not give them to you lightly and you may be refused your request," said Math.

"My plan is not a bad one lord," explained Gwydion, "and we will not return without the swine in our possession."

"You have my leave to go then," said Math.

Gwydion, Gilfaethwy and the ten others then rode out to Ceredigion to Rhuddlan Teifi, which was Pryderi's court in that part of his domain. The twelve then disguised themselves as bards and requested to enter the court. They were received joyfully and a feast began, with Gwydion sitting to one side of Pryderi and everyone else according to their rank.

"We will gladly hear a story from one of your bards," Pryderi said to Gwydion.

"It is customary among us lord that the first to speak in a host's court is the head bard himself, I will gladly tell you a story." Gwydion stood and began to speak.

He was the greatest storyteller everyone had ever heard and the court was soon praising him for his entertaining tales. When he finished Pryderi was glad to talk to him and Gwydion saw his chance.

"Would there be any other man here in a better position to ask a request from you?" he asked Pwyll.

"There would not, for you have the gift of eloquence with you." answered Pryderi.

"Then I request from you the swine that were given to you by Arawn."

"That would be an easy request to give, but I have promised my people that I will keep them until they have bred twice their number," said Pwyll.

"It will not be hard to overcome that promise," said Gwydion, "do not refuse me tonight and I will come to you tomorrow with an offer for them."

That night they went to their lodgings and Gwydion, by use of his magic, conjured up twelve stallions and twelve greyhounds, all with fine collars and leashes. Anyone that looked at the animals would have thought that their saddles and collars were made from pure gold. Gwydion brought the animals to Pryderi the next day.

"Lord, would you give the pigs to me for these fine gifts? Your people will see that you have not sold them but exchanged them for gifts with more value." said Gwydion.

Pryderi decided to hold a council and everyone agreed that he should exchange the animals. Gwydion took them and immediately hurried back to Gwynedd for he knew that his magic would not last long. He built a sty for the pigs in Arllechwedd and then went to see Math at Caer Dathal. There they found that the men of Gwynedd were being mustered for the news had already reached Math that Pryderi was preparing the cantrefs of Dyfed against him in war. Math asked after the animals and when he heard they were safe he went with his forces to face Pryderi.

Everything had gone according to plan and Gwydion and Gilfaethwy stayed behind in Caer Dathal. That night Gilfaethwy took Math's foot maiden Goewin against her will.

The brothers rose the next day and set out after Math. The forces of Gwynedd were waiting between the towns of Pennarth and Coed Alun. Pryderi attacked and there was inflicted great slaughter on both sides until Pryderi and the men of the south were forced to retreat and muster their forces. Another battle took place after they rallied until, after countless deaths, the men of Dyfed eventually sought a truce and gave hostages to Math.

Math's army then escorted Pryderi's forces southward through Gwynedd but the two sides soon could not be stopped from attacking each other, so great was their bitterness about their losses. Pryderi sent a messenger to Math asking that the forces should be separated and that Gwydion, the cause of the war, should meet him in personal combat. Math agreed to this for he did not want the two armies to fight needlessly.

Pryderi and Gwydion armed themselves and fought. They were equals in combat but by virtue of his magic and enchantments Gwydion was the victor and Pryderi the ruler of Dyfed was killed. His men buried him with great sorrow at Maen Tyryawg above Y Felen Rhyd. Then they set off homewards weeping bitterly for they had lost their lord and a great number of their men. They were glad when their hostages returned after them unharmed, but it did not cure all their pain.

So Pryderi son of Pwyll died through the trickery and magic of Gwydion. His death however does not go wholly unavenged as Math soon finds out about the rape of his footmaiden Goewin. After marrying Goewin Math punishes Gwydion and Gilfaethwy for the rape and for causing the slaughter and needless death of Pryderi. He strikes the two nephews with his magic staff turning Gilfaethwy into a hind and Gwydion into a stag. The two then go to the wild and mate like animals. When they come back with their offspring Math turns them into a boar and a sow. They mate again and give birth to a pig and are then turned into a wolf and a she-wolf. When they give birth to a cub Math decides they have been shamed enough and restores them to human form.

Pryderi's death is not all due to the power of Gwydion though and he cannot himself be absolved of all blame. The pigs that Arawn gave to Pwyll or Pryderi are one of the main factors that leads to his death. The magical pigs must have been a source of wealth to Pryderi and his people and he shows poor judgement when he gives them away for earthly riches. It seems an ironic end to the story of Pryderi that he dies through his misjudgement in giving away his pigs when it was his father's good judgement that had earned them in the first place.

It may seem strange to us that in the story Math had never heard of pigs before but in Celtic tradition it was thought that some domestic animals originated in the Otherworld. Pig meat was a great luxury in Celtic society and so legends like the one of Pwyll and Arawn were created to account for this great gift to mankind. Pigs also seem to have a special relationship with the area of Pembrokeshire. Pryderi is named in a triad as one of the 'Three Powerful Swineherds of the island of Britain' who guards the swine of Pendaren Dyfed in Glyn Cuch, the same forest in Cilgerran where Pwyll met Arawn. Pembrokeshire is also an important part in the legend of the giant boar Twrch Trwyth whom we will encounter in chapter three.

Pryderi's large role in the four branches of the Mabinogion led the important Celtic scholar W. J. Gruffydd to arrive at the conclusion that the four branches were originally all concerned with the hero

37

Pryderi. In early Irish literature there are four important parts in the lives of heroes, the conception, the youthful exploits, the banishment or imprisonment, and finally the death of the hero. The story as we have it now holds traces of such an arrangement but many pieces are not there. The birth tale is given in full but Pryderi is only briefly mentioned as one of the survivors from Ireland in the second branch, in the third branch his friend Manawydan is the main character and his death, as we have seen, forms only part of the story of Math and Gwydion.

Gruffydd's argument is possible but it seems likely that as Pryderi plays such a small part in the other stories the Mabinogion was never just about his life. Pryderi's part is probably that of a unifying strand through the complexities of all the four branches. His fame as a hero in Pembrokeshire was well known to the medieval Welsh poets of the middle ages, one of whom refers to Dyfed as 'Pryderi's land'. It is possible that he was once an important character in other heroic legends. By comparison his father Pwyll is an obscure character, possibly invented for the Mabinogion as father of Pryderi Lord of Dyfed.

The place of Pryderi's burial, given in the story above, is found in the Black Book of Carmarthen that was written somewhere in Dyfed around the same time or possibly earlier than the Mabinogion. In this book, in the verses known as the Beddau Stanzas or 'Grave Poems', it is stated that:

"In Aber Gwenoli
lies the grave of Pryderi,
where the waves
strike the land.

(Trans: Meirion Pennar)

Aber Gwenoli is the same place mentioned in the Mabinogion, at Maen Tyryawg, where the stream Gwenoli runs into the river Y Felenrhyd. This is near Portmeirion in Gwynedd, far away from his birthplace and his lands at Arberth, a sad ending to the tales of Pwyll and Pryderi.

# Manawydan Son of Llyr

Although we have left him dead and buried we must now briefly revive Pryderi to hear of the trials of his companion Manawydan. 'Manawydan Son of Llyr' is the third branch of the Mabinogi and like the first branch it takes place in Pembrokeshire. It follows on from the story of the disastrous expedition to Ireland to rescue Bran's daughter, Branwen. Manawydan, Pryderi and the five other survivors of the battle mournfully bury the head of Bran in London and then find that Caswallawn has usurped Bran's kingship of Britain in his absence. Manawydan, being Bran's brother, should have inherited the throne but his cousin Caswallawn has killed the men who were left to guard Britain and taken his inheritance by force.

Manawydan however will not fight with Caswallawn for his right to rule and he will not even ask him to grant him land saying that he does not like seeing anyone in Bran's place. Pryderi, seeing Manawydan's dire situation offers him the seven cantrefs of Dyfed and his mother Rhiannon to be his bride. Manawydan asks if he can first see Rhiannon and the land he has been offered and so we join the story as they decide to return home to Dyfed.

Manawydan and Pryderi journeyed back to Dyfed to find that Rhiannon and Cigfa, Pryderi's wife, had prepared a feast for them. They sat down to eat and Manawydan was introduced to Rhiannon. They both talked through the night and soon enough both became fond of the other. Pryderi told his mother Rhiannon about the offer he had made Manawydan and she accepted this gladly. Manwaydan also accepted Pryderi's kind offer and before the night was over the couple had slept together.

The next morning Pryderi decided to set out and offer his homage to the king Caswallawn but Rhiannon said that he was in Kent and so Pryderi waited for Caswallawn to travel nearer. Because of this the four feasted again and for another day enjoyed each other's company. Afterwards they went on a circuit of Dyfed and were delighted to see the land so plentiful and well stocked with honey and fish. They then heard that Caswallawn was in Oxford so Pryderi went there to offer his submission, which Caswallawn received with great thanks.

When he returned Manawydan, Rhiannon and Cigfa continued to feast at the court of Arberth. After the first evening had passed they all decided to go to the Mound of Arberth, the mound of wonders. Before they even reached the mound though they heard a great clap of thunder and a mist descended across the land so thick that no one could even see their companions. When this mist lifted they looked over the land. Where there had previously been dwellings, animals and people all they saw was empty countryside.

When they returned to the court all they found were deserted buildings with not a man or animal in sight. They were obviously troubled by this but decided to keep their spirits up by preparing another feast and travelling around the land to search for some sign of life. They still had each other's company but all they could find in the whole of Dyfed was wild beasts. They managed to spend a year together in Dyfed and when their stores ran out they hunted and lived off the land's plentiful fish and honey.

After another year passed they grew weary of Dyfed's emptiness and decided to go to England to practice a trade. First they settled in Hereford where they made saddles and they were soon so skilled at it that everyone who wanted one bought it from them. The other saddlemakers became jealous and they all got together and decided to kill their rivals. Pryderi and Manawydan heard of this and Pryderi felt so angry he wanted to kill the other saddlemakers. Manawydan however knew that if they did kill them they would lose their honour and go to prison so they decided to go and seek another trade elsewhere.

In the next city they took up shieldmaking. They copied the fine shields they had seen back home and soon enough everyone in the town bought their shields from them. The other shieldmakers were angry with this for they were not selling any of their produce and so they plotted to kill their competitors. Pryderi and Manawydan soon heard of these plans. Again Pryderi wanted to kill them but Manawydan was afraid that if they did Caswallawn would hear of it and give them great trouble, so they decided to move to another town.

In the next city they thought of taking up saddlemaking or shieldmaking again because they already knew these crafts but Manawydan decided to take up shoemaking instead, thinking that the other shoemakers would not be bold enough to plot to kill them.

40

They bought the best leather in the town and Manawydan went to the best goldsmith in the town to have their buckles guilded. Manawydan watched the goldsmith at work and soon learned how to guild shoes himself and for this he became known as one of the Three Golden Shoemakers. Soon enough everyone was coming to him to buy their shoes and the other shoemakers became angry and decided to kill the strangers but again Manawydan heard of this. Pryderi wanted to kill them more than he had wanted to kill the others but Manawydan thought it better for them to return to Dyfed rather than fight.

When they returned to Dyfed they lived off the land as they had done before. Pryderi and Manawydan hunted with their dogs and they passed a year like this. One day while they were hunting the dogs broke away from them and headed towards a small copse of trees. When the dogs reached the trees they returned quickly to the horses and, trembling with fear, they refused to move ahead any further.

"We should ride over there and see what has frightened our dogs," said Pryderi.

But as they neared the copse a shining white boar burst out and started running away. The men urged the dogs after it but the boar would just bait and fight the dogs until the men arrived, then it would run further away and wait for the dogs again.

The white boar stayed ahead of the men like this for some time until they came to a tall fortress. The boar entered the fortress and the dogs followed quickly after it. Pryderi and Manawydan stopped to marvel at the magnificent castle that stood where there had previously only been bare ground. They listened for the dogs barking but could hear nothing.

"Lord," said Pryderi to Manawydan, "I will enter the fortress and find the dogs."

"That is not a good idea," answered Manawydan, "for I am sure that whoever has enchanted Dyfed is also responsible for this fortress. If you would take my advice you would not enter it for you will surely come to harm."

"I will not give up my dogs," said Pryderi and, ignoring the advice, he entered the castle. Inside he could not see his dogs, the boar or any other man, beast or dwelling. All he could see was a marble fountain in the middle of the fortress. Over this fountain

41

was a golden bowl fastened to four chains that extended into the air so far that he could not see the ends of them. He was curious about this and went over to inspect the bowl. It was the finest crafted bowl that he had ever seen and he was so enamoured by it that he reached out to touch its rim. As soon as he did this his hand stuck to the bowl, his feet stuck to the marble floor and his speech was taken away from him. He could do nothing but stand there in silence.

Outside Manawydan waited and waited until evening. When he saw that he would hear no news of Pryderi or the dogs he returned to the court and told Rhiannon all that had happened.

"Shame on you," she said, "you have been a bad companion and have lost a dear friend," and with that she left for the castle.

Reaching the fortress she entered through the open gate and immediately she saw her son standing by the golden bowl.

"What are you doing here my son," she asked but then she too grabbed the bowl and became stuck to the slab.

With that a clap of thunder rolled across the land and a thick mist fell. By the time it lifted the fortress was gone and Pryderi and Rhiannon with it.

Cigfa became very distressed at this for now only she and Manawydan remained in the whole of Dyfed. She began to lament that living like they were was no better than being dead.

"Do not weep through despair," comforted Manawydan, "between me and God you have no truer friend than I. I will give you friendship as long as it is in my power to do so until this misery is lifted from us."

"That is what I had hoped," said Cigfa and she took courage from this friendship.

"We cannot stay here any longer," said Manawydan, "for we have lost our dogs and cannot hunt. We should go to England for it will be easier there."

"I will gladly go, but what craft will you take?" asked Cigfa.

"I will take no other craft than shoemaking, for that is what I am best at," said Manawydan.

"But that is not pure enough for your rank and talents," protested Cigfa.

"That may be so," said Manawydan, "but it is what I shall do," and so they set out for England.

After they arrived he was soon making shoes from the best leather in town and the other shoemakers work failed to even compare with the quality of his shoes. After they had been there a year all the people of the town came to them for shoes and, as in all the other towns, the other shoemakers became very jealous. They joined together and plotted to kill him but Manawydan soon heard of this plan.

"We should not tolerate this," said Cigfa.

"We will not," answered Manawydan, "so we will return to Dyfed."

Manawydan first gathered some wheat together and then they set out for Dyfed once more. They were both very pleased to see Arberth again and remembered the good times they had spent here with Rhiannon and Pryderi. They soon settled there with Manawydan hunting fish and gathering honey to support them. He tilled three fields and in each of them planted some of the wheat he had brought with him from England. The wheat grew into a fine crop and Manawydan waited out the seasons until it was ripe. When it came to harvest time he went out to one of the fields and looked at his crop.

"I will reap this one tomorrow," he said, seeing that the field had ripened.

He spent the night at Arberth and when dawn came he set out to reap the field but when he arrived at the field all he found was the broken stalks of his crop. All of the wheat had been taken away in the space of one night. He was surprised at this and went to his other fields but luckily they were untouched. Noticing that one of these fields was ready for harvesting he decided to harvest it the next day.

He awoke at dawn ready to harvest the second field but again all he found was a field full of broken stalks with not an ear of wheat in sight.

"The person who started my destruction has come back to complete it," he said to himself.

"My last crop is ready for reaping and I will be shamed if I do not stay here and wait for whoever has been destroying my crops for they will surely come tonight for this one."

Manawydan gathered his weapons and sat guard over the crop. When midnight came he heard the loudest noise he had ever heard in his life. He could not tell where the noise was coming from until he saw a host of mice approaching. They were all around him squeaking and rustling and were more numerous than the drops of water in the ocean. Each mouse broke off one ear of wheat and carried it away between its teeth and soon enough all of the mice were carrying an ear. His anger and frustration at this was great and he ran into them hacking and slashing but it would have been easier for him to stop the rain by hitting each rain drop than to stop the mice.

Eventually he noticed one little mouse that was fatter than the others. It moved slowly and so he was able to chase and catch it. He put the mouse into one of his gloves and tied the end tightly with string.

With the thief in his pocket he returned to Arberth and hung the glove up by the fireplace in Cigfa's chamber.

"What's in there?" she enquired. Manawydan told her what had happened to his crops and how he had caught the mouse.

"What are you going to do with it?" she asked.

"It is a thief so I will hang it tomorrow," he answered.

"But lord, it is not fitting for a man of your standing to be dealing with such a lowly creature. My advice would be for you to let it go," said Cigfa.

"It is a shame that I did not catch them all, for they would have been hanged. As it is I intend to hang the one I did catch," said Manawydan.

"I only thought to ask you to let it go so that you would keep your honour lord," said Cigfa.

"If I knew a good reason why you should plead for its release I would take your advice but as you have no reason I intend to punish the creature," said Manawydan.

"Very well lord," said Cigfa.

The next day Manawydan set out for The Mound of Arberth with the mouse still in the glove. On top of the mound he placed two forks of wood in the ground, intending to hang the mouse between them. As he was doing so he saw a scholar dressed in tattered and shabby clothes coming towards him, the first person he had seen in Dyfed apart from his companions for many years.

"Good day!" said the scholar.

"God's blessing to you," answered Manawydan, "Where are you

going?"

"I have come from singing in England, why do you ask?" asked the scholar.

"I have not seen anyone except for my dear companions here for the last seven years," explained Manawydan. "so you are the first stranger I have seen in all that time."

"I am just passing through here on my way back to my own lands lord. What are you doing on this mound?" the scholar asked.

"I have caught a thief and I intend to hang it," answered Manawydan.

"But you have a mouse in your hand!" exclaimed the scholar, "It is not fitting for a man of your rank to be seen handling such a lowly creature."

"That may be true," said Manawydan, "but I intend to hang it anyway."

"I will save you from this embarrassment," answered the scholar, "I have a pound I earned while singing, I will give it to you if you let the creature loose."

"Between me and God I will not do that," answered Manawydan.

"Well, I only thought to help you lord, now I must go."

The scholar left and Manawydan placed a stick between the forks. As he did this he saw a priest approach him on a fine horse. The priest greeted him and asked what he was doing and Manawydan replied as he had done before. The priest offered three pounds for the mouse in order to save Manawydan's honour but Manawydan would still not let the mouse go and so the priest rode off.

Manawydan then drew some string around the mouse's neck and as he did so a retinue of horses and men approached him. Behind the retinue a bishop appeared and came up to Manwaydan.

"I ask your blessing bishop," said Manawydan.

"God grants a blessing to you lord," said the Bishop, "What are you doing there?"

"I am hanging a thief," replied Manawydan.

"But you have a mouse in your hand!"

"The mouse is the thief," said Manawydan, "and I intend to hang him."

"It is not right for a man of your nobility to do such a thing. I will buy the mouse off you for seven pounds," said the bishop.

"Between me and God I will not sell it," answered Manawydan.

"If you will not sell it for that I will give you twenty four pounds to let it go," said the bishop.

"I will not sell it for double that amount," said Manawydan.

"If you will not accept money I will offer you all the horses and baggage I have here with me if you will let the mouse go," said the bishop.

"Between me and God I will not sell the mouse for that," said Manawydan.

"If you will not give me the mouse for that then I ask you to name your price," said the bishop.

"I want the release of Rhiannon and Pryderi," answered Manawydan.

"You shall have that," replied the bishop.

"That is not all," said Manawydan, "I want the enchantment lifted from Dyfed."

"You shall have that too, now release the mouse."

"That is not all, I want to know who the mouse is," said Manawydan.

"She is my wife," said the bishop, "that is why I am ransoming her."

"How did she come to me?" asked Manawydan.

"She came to plunder," said the bishop, "I am Llwyd son of Cil Coed and it was I who enchanted Dyfed in revenge for the game of Badger in the Bag played by Pwyll on my friend Gwawl at the court of Hefeydd the Old. When I heard you had returned to Dyfed I sent my men as mice to steal your crops for two nights. On the third night the ladies of the court came also to ask to be turned into mice so I granted them that. My pregnant wife was with them and she is the fat mouse you hold in your hand. If she were not with them you would not have caught anyone, but as you have, I come to ransom her. I have told you who the mouse is so release her."

"I shall not release her until you give me your word that you will never put an enchantment on the cantrefs of Dyfed again," said Manawydan.

"I will do that," said the bishop, "now release her."

"I will not do that," said Manawydan, "You must also give your word that you will never take revenge on Pryderi, Rhiannon or myself because of this."

"I will do that and it was a good thing you asked for that," said Llwyd, "because otherwise more harm than this would have come to you and Dyfed. Now release my wife."

"I will not do that," said Manawydan, "until I see Rhiannon and Pryderi coming towards me."

"You shall have that," said the bishop.

Pryderi and Rhiannon appeared and Manawydan rose to greet his friends warmly and they were all glad to see one another.

"Now release my wife," asked Llwyd, so Manawydan untied the mouse and Llwyd struck it with a magic wand, turning it back into a lovely young woman who was heavy with child.

"Look around you now," said Llwyd, "and you will see that the curse has been lifted from your land and all my promises have been kept," said Llwyd.

Manawydan and the others then saw that all the beasts, houses and people had returned to the country, for they had not been destroyed but had been hidden from view, and so Dyfed was finally complete once more.

Thus ends this Branch of the Mabinogi.

It is Llwyd then who is behind Dyfed's desolation in revenge for the time that Pwyll beat his friend Gwawl in the first Mabinogi. It may seem strange that he takes his revenge on Pryderi after Pwyll is long dead but grievances in Celtic society involved the whole family rather than the individual and so Llwyd was taking his rightful revenge on Pwyll's son and wife. There are also subtle similarities between this story and Pwyll's as in this story Llwyd was defeated after his wife was captured in a bag-like glove and in Pwyll's story Gwawl was captured and defeated in Rhiannon's magic bag.

This story, like Pwyll's, can also be seen as another 'teaching tale'. Manawydan lost his claim to inherit his brother's kingdom after Caswallawn took it, then he lost all the people from his newly acquired land of Dyfed and finally he loses his friend and wife. All the way through these trials he shows a level of patience and understanding that sometimes borders on complacency. This is the only branch of the Mabinogi where no one dies and through Manawydan's refusal to resort to violence and his patient attitude he eventually wins back his friends and the productivity of his land.

The storyteller may be reinforcing the point that patience and abstention from unnecessary violence are as important to a king as strength and wisdom. The patient and peaceful nature of Manawydan in the story could also portray the character of the writer who may have been a man of the church. This image of a wise Manawydan is also found in an early poem where he is described as Manawydan 'whose council was wealthy'. The peaceful side to Manawydan portrayed in the Mabinogion was probably a later development however as the next line of the same poem describes how he brought 'shattered shields back from battle'.

Manawydan, although favoured by the writer of the Mabinogi, still appears as quite a weak character. He loses his inheritance of the kingship of Britain to Caswallawn and does not seem bothered. Pryderi has to offer him part of his own kingdom out of charity which therefore reduced Manawydan to the rank of a sub-lord. When he does rule over this land it becomes desolate and infertile after just one day of his leadership, even though, like Pwyll, he had united with Rhiannon, the goddess of the land. Because Rhiannon normally assures the lands fertility it is therefore implied that he himself is infertile. It is also Rhiannon who goes to the castle to find Pryderi while Manawydan just stays home. After he has lost his wife Manawydan goes to England to work as a craftsman even though he is a Lord. When he returns to Dyfed with his wheat seeds he becomes a farmer and when he fails to even grow a crop he finally takes his last step down the social ladder and ends up as a mouse catcher, hardly a fitting occupation for the rightful king of Britain.

Whereas the first branch is about how Pwyll becomes a just and wise king ruling over a fertile land this branch is about how a king loses his land, fertility and honour through complacency and unkingly actions. Even if the storyteller gives Manawydan back his lands and friends at the end of the story this does not change the fact that he had already lost everything. The main features of Celtic kingship were the king's honour and his land's fertility. Manawydan slowly loses all the things that make him a king and he ends up as an example of an anti-king.

The scholar John Koch, in a recent study, discovered something else which is very important, and surprising, to the story of Manawydan. To understand this we have to first go back to Roman

48

times and to Caesar's account in his book 'The Gallic Wars' of the Roman invasion of Britain in 54 BC. The leader of the Britons against the Romans is Cassivellaunos, the same person as Caswallawn in the Mabinogi who takes the kingship from Manawydan's brother Bran. The similarities do not end there for the story of Cassivellaunos in 'The Gallic Wars' has other parallels in the story of Manawydan.

In his book Caesar says that when he invaded Cassivellaunos was elected as leader over all of the Britons. Soon an army from all over Britain assembled at Kent under Cassivellaunos. In the Mabinogi Pryderi goes to Kent to pay homage to Caswallawn after he becomes ruler of all Britain. In the Gallic Wars after his first defeat Cassivellaunos starts using guerrilla warfare against Caesar and to confuse the Roman army he hides all of the animals and people wherever Caesar marched. In the Mabinogi, soon after Pryderi meets Caswallawn all of Dyfed's animals and people disappear. In the Gallic wars to counter the guerrilla tactics Caesar starts to burn all the crops he comes across and likewise in the Mabinogi Manawydan's crops of corn disappear in the night.

The similarities are increased when we look at Mandubracius, Manawydan's counterpart in 'The Gallic Wars'. Mandubracius was a prince of the Trinovantes tribe who, after his father was killed by Cassivellaunos fled in exile to Gaul. In the Mabinogi it is Manawydan's cousin who is deposed by Caswallawn and later dies from grief. Manawydan also goes to England in exile after Dyfed is cursed and so it seems that Mandubracius and Manawydan are similar characters with similar backgrounds in both the Gallic Wars and the Mabinogi branch

It is the main plot in both books that is most important. In the Gallic wars the Trinovante tribe side with Caesar and ask for Mandubracius to be installed as their leader. This Caesar grants in exchange for hostages and a supply of corn for his army. While this is happening Cassivellaunos's hillfort is attacked and won by the Romans but Cassivellaunos is still not captured. Some tribes still loyal to him attacked the Roman beach head in Kent but they failed and a noble called Lugotorix is taken hostage. When Cassivellaunos hears of this he asks Caesar for peace. Caesar accepts but Cassivellaunus must give him hostages and send a yearly tribute to Caesar. He also has to promise not to do any harm

49

to Mandubracius.

These final events are the key to the two stories. In the Gallic Wars Caesar captures Lugotorix and Cassivellaunos sues for peace, in the Mabinogi Manawydan captures a mouse and Llwyd sues for peace. Then in the Gallic Wars Caesar makes Cassivellaunos swear that he will not harm Mandubracius and in the Mabinogi Manawydan makes Llwyd swear that he will not harm himself, Pryderi or Rhiannon. After peace was made with Cassivellaunos presumably all of the people and animals that had been hidden in Britain would have been returned just as they were in Dyfed when Llwyd released the spell. It is also very fitting that the name of Caesar's hostage, Lugotorix, could easily be confused as meaning 'mouse king'.

Cassivellaunos or Caswallawn would have probably been in the place of Llwyd in an earlier form of the story and if this is done then the end of Manawydan and the end of the account in The Gallic wars are remarkably similar. Mandubracius is another anti-king figure just like Manawydan, both lose their right to inherit kingship through the actions of Cassivellaunus/Caswallawn and both take flight to foreign countries. Mandubracius and Manawydan are also both restored as rulers but only after they have lost their right to proper kingship.

Supporters of Cassivellaunos must have formed the story of Mandubracius and Manawydan after Caesar's war in Britain. The story then, as it is now, must have been a cautionary tale about the loss of the divine right of kingship. It is remarkable that Caesar's account and the Mabinogi story which are separated by 1300 years should be so similar. An important point is that the writer of the Mabinogi did not merely read Caesar's account and use this as his source because it was not available to him in the middle ages. He was therefore drawing on the story as it was found in native Welsh tradition where the tale of Manawydan the anti-king must have been told by storytellers in various forms for over a thousand years. This survival is a vivid and striking testimony to the strength and endurance of the oral tradition of the Celts and to the rich cultural background of the Mabinogi.

Oral tradition is organic and as well as retaining certain elements it also changes and adapts over time. In Welsh tradition the figure of Manawydan soon evolved away from the iron age king

Mandubracius. He was confused very early on with the Irish god Manannan son of Lir who appears as the ruler of an Otherworld island and also gave his name to the Isle of Man. The Irish Manannan was a sea god and 'son of Lir' means literally 'son of the sea'. Manawydan thus also gained the same title in Welsh of 'son of Llyr' but Manawydan has no similarities with Manannan or the sea. It seems to have merely been the similarity of the names that made people associate the Welsh figure with the Irish one.

Manawydan appears in two of the Welsh triads, both which are related to the Mabinogi story. He is one of the 'Three Prostrate Chieftains' who were subdued by misfortune and had failed to gain the land that was their right. He is also one of the 'Three Golden Shoemakers of the Island of Britain' which refers to his stay in England as a craftsman. This association of Manawydan with shoes probably arose because of the similarity of his name with 'manawyd', the Welsh word for 'awl', a tool used in shoemaking. This shows that legends and myths could be altered by many different factors and that it was easy for them to evolve. Strangely enough Caswallawn is himself another of the shoemakers in the triad but the source of this story has unfortunately not survived. Was he too an anti-king figure in another lost tale?

The story of Manawydan is rich in magical themes all of which come from Welsh tradition. The fortress that appears to Pryderi and Manawydan is an Otherworld castle, which probably belongs to Llwyd. The white boar that leads them to the castle is a similar figure to the white dogs in the story of Pwyll. This white animal is the bridge that carries Pryderi and Manawydan from the real world into the magical Otherworld castle. Inside the fortress the golden bowl over the fountain is another appearance of the 'Cauldron of Plenty'. This cauldron appears in the Mabinogi branch of Branwen where it is used to bring dead warriors back to life. These warriors however cannot speak afterwards, just as Pryderi and Rhiannon, when they touch the bowl, lose their speech. This symbol of the cauldron or fountain appears throughout Celtic tradition and will also appear again in this book in a Pembrokeshire folktale.

With all these references to Caesar and cauldrons it is easy to lose sight of Pembrokeshire's part in the story. The fact that two Mabinogi branches take place in the county show its position of prime importance in both medieval legend and society. The mound

51

at Arberth was a magical place which appears in this story to illustrate Manawydan's weakness. Whereas when Pwyll sits on the mound he meets Rhiannon the goddess of sovereignty, Manawydan loses all the people and animals of all of Dyfed before he even reaches the mound. This is another indication of Manawydan's role as the un-king, for even the magical mound at the centre of his realm fails to give him a wonder. The mound in fact is used as a hanging place for a mouse by Manawydan and in Dewsland there is the suggestive place name of Knuck y Llygod, 'The Mice Mound', but unfortunately this could easily refer to the real animals and not to Llwyd's transformed wife.

Apart from these references to the court of Arberth there is one other place-name given at the end of the story that relates to Pembrokeshire. After Pryderi and Rhiannon are freed Manawydan asks Llwyd how they have been imprisoned. Llwyd answers that Pryderi wore the gate-hammers of the court and Rhiannon wore the collars of the asses after they had carried the hay. These strange actions are given as the translation of the story's other, perhaps older, name of the 'Mabinogi Mynweir a Mynordd'. It has been suggested that these names represent the villages of Mynwear and Manordean in Pembrokeshire. Manordean is a village in Cilgerran and Mynwear, a word that could be thought of as meaning 'Hay-neck', is a village not far from Arberth. The name of the Mabinogi branch was probably an ancient one that was not understood by the medieval writer of the Mabinogi. It does show however that localities in Pembrokeshire may once have been more involved in the plot than they are now.

The ancient kingdom of Dyfed centred around Arberth appears in the Mabinogi as a prime example of a Welsh kingship. The kings and the princes who listened to the stories would have heard the tale of Dyfed's great king Pwyll and then Dyfed's anti-king Manawydan. Both stories would have stood as cautionary tales of how a kingdom is won or lost. It must be remembered however that the story of the kingship of Dyfed ended with Pryderi's violent death in the war with Gwynedd, perhaps reinforcing the reality that kings, no matter how well they rule, often meet with violent deaths. This aspect of the Mabinogion as a teaching tool was important because the continued re-telling of these traditional tales would have reflected and reinforced the values and aspirations of medieval Welsh society.

## Chapter Two

## The Age of Saints

We must now leave the tales of the Celtic gods and heroes and turn our attention to another important part of medieval Welsh history. The age of the saints was the period from when the Romans left Britain until Christianity became established in the seventh to ninth centuries AD. These 'dark age' centuries earned this name because most of the literary and archaeological evidence for this whole period concerns the early saints and their settlements. Many stories of the saints legendary lives survive from middle age manuscripts and together with church dedications and early inscribed stones they give us valuable information on where and when these early Christians first settled.

This was a time of great change in Wales. The Romans had recently departed and the religion of Britain was a mixture of pagan Celtic tradition and early Roman Christianity that had come from the continent. The changes this new religion brought to society must have been slow and gradual, as there are no traditions of conflict or persecutions. The Christian beliefs were slowly adopted into Celtic society until Wales, like the other western Celtic countries, had developed an established church. In the eyes of the people the saints themselves seem to have adopted some of the characteristics of the magicians and druids of the past. Soon after they died they were often credited with miraculous and legendary lives which are very similar to the mythical tales of the pagan gods and heroes told before them.

Christianity first came to Britain largely through the migrations from southern Gaul of Romano-Christians who were escaping both the collapse of Roman order and the threat of barbarian invasion. They travelled from the continent using the well-used sea routes to Britain and their early settlements are shown by the evidence of their Latin Christian funeral slabs. These stones have a high concentration in Pembrokeshire which shows how important the area was to the beginnings of the Celtic Church in Britain. These Christians soon spread their settlements inland throughout Pembrokeshire using the established route that started at Porth Clais at St Davids and followed the old Roman road eastward through lowland south Wales to the Severn estuary. As well as Romano-Christianity another form of Christianity came to Britain that looked to the asceticism of the east. These Christians thought it better to pray to God by seeking a solitary life free from material desires and in Britain not only did they find many lonely places but they also found a largely unconverted population.

The Welsh church that was created by these early followers was throughout its life in direct contact with Ireland, Cornwall and Brittany. The closeness between these countries cannot be underestimated for they were in direct communication with each other through the sea, the only efficient travel method of the era. By using the seas the saints could travel freely and so they could preach in Ireland one year and be on a pilgrimage to Rome the next. In this way ideas spread easily and the many different parts of the Celtic Church were able to keep in regular contact with each other.

Although they travelled, each saint generally became known in the particular area where his or her influence was strongest. St Brynach for example is closely associated with an area of Cemais in north-east Pembrokeshire where there are many places named after him. The largely coastal position of the whole county meant that Pembrokeshire was a major thoroughfare for saints travelling all over the Celtic lands. Because of this a large number and variety of settlements developed, not all of which were originally Welsh. There are churches in Pembrokeshire that were established by travellers like St Patrick and St Colman from Ireland and St Petroc from Cornwall.

Inscribed stones and 'clas' churchyards form the archaeological evidence for the lives of these early Christians. The clas churchyards are small and circular and usually mark the early settlement where the original saint would have first built a small cell or oratory. The early inscribed stones are also found in connection with these and were usually decorated with crosses and Latin inscriptions. These were originally either gravestones or were used in the clas as a focal point for meetings and worship or as the saint's altar. These crosses are usually still to be found in modern churchyards illustrating the length of time that these sites have been used.

There is an abundance of these settlements, founded by the early wandering saints in Pembrokeshire. These saints spent much of

55

their time alone in solace with God but they also preached and spread the word of God with vigour, founding many small chapels and churches for the local population. Because of the dangerous times they chose their settlements well, usually siting them on the coast but out of sight behind cliffs or around river bends. St Davids was sited in the valley behind a bend on the river Alun and even the tall spire of the cathedral can only be seen when you are very close to it. The coast offered good communications but it also brought the dangers of invaders and pirates. Islands were also chosen by the early saints as they offered solitude and although separated from normal mainland life they were also close enough for missionary contact.

Many early Christian settlements used existing pagan ritual sites for their religious foundations, giving them a continuity from the past and the inherited authority to represent the beliefs of the people. The early chapels and churches are often associated with sacred wells and megaliths proving that this earlier religious sanctity was an factor in where the early Christians settled. In many cases the existing traditions of the local people must have been very strong with the old rituals adapted and altered rather than changed outright. An example of this is at holy wells where the saints often replaced the old pagan deity of the well to became the protectors of the holy waters, mirroring rather than destroying the peoples beliefs. This re-invention of many pagan sites kept many of the ancient beliefs active throughout the following centuries and preserved some aspects of the old sacred landscape.

This age of saints happened well over a thousand years ago, so for many of these early saints all that remains of their life and work are a few scattered church dedications. We can however sometimes get a brief glimpse of these lost characters from the church names. Llanrheithian is dedicated to a Rheithan whose name probably means 'Man of Law' and nearby is Llanrhian dedicated to Rhian whose name means 'Little King'. The name of Llanddinog similarly points to a personal name meaning 'Talented' or 'One of Outstanding Gifts'. These names give us an indication of the high social status of many of the saints but many other saints names like St Tygigai of Llandigige-Fawr, St Elfyw of St Elvis and St Hywel of Llanhowel are all now unknown.

The earliest direct written evidence for the church in

Pembrokeshire comes from the tenth century and gives the names of four churches with important status. These were St Davids, St Ishmaels, Llan Degeman (now Rhoscrowther) and St Issells. There were also other important foundations like the monasteries of Caldey Island, St Dogmaels and the mother church at Penally. These places were patronised by the local rulers who sent their young men to the monks and priests to be trained in reading, writing and religion. Many of the pupils who taught under the great early teachers then left the monasteries to become saints themselves, spreading the gospels even further.

Only the few early saints who gained a wide renown had 'Lives' written about them in the middle ages and fewer still had folk traditions about them which until recently survived in Pembrokeshire. The later notoriety of all the saints lay not so much in their deeds and actions while they were alive but how their settlements grew over time and the ways in which their traditions were kept alive by the local people. It will be easy to see at the end of this chapter that the differences between the churches of St David and St Gofan lies not in the saints' fame and piety while they were alive but in how their churches and lands fared later on in the middle ages.

The surviving evidence of the settlement and traditions of the early saints in Pembrokeshire is rich and varied and it illustrates this interesting period very well. The saints got up to a lot more than setting up churches and worshipping God as the story of Aidan and Gwynda will show. The two saints, who were on their way to St Davids at the time, stopped at the well called Fynnon Tregroes in Whitchurch. They both wished to name the well after themselves and so they argued and argued about which one of them it should be dedicated to. Aidan soon lost his patience and proceeded to beat up Gwynda! When he had done this he dedicated the well to himself and carried on his way to St Davids. The first saint we will look at in this chapter is a very famous one who was not at all violent. In fact it was his peaceful nature that was famed in the middle ages and his life is still celebrated every year by the people of Wales.

# St David

St David, called Dewi Sant in Welsh, is the patron saint of Wales. He was born in Pembrokeshire and spent his life working all around west Wales, founding the country's most renowned monastical seat as early as the sixth century AD. The Annals of Wales say he was born in 458 AD but other sources say it was in 520 AD. Not all the dates and stories told about his life can be believed though for after his death his life was turned into a legend about the establishment of Celtic Christianity in the pagan lands of Pembrokeshire.

The 'Life of St David', where this story is from, was written by Rhigyfarch, a son of a renowned bishop of St Davids, around 1090. During this period the Normans were pressing on the lands of the Welsh princes and the book was written to further the independence of St Davids from Canterbury. Another factor behind the book's creation may also have been the visit by William the Conqueror to Dewi's sanctuary in 1081 when peace was made between him and Rhys ap Tewdwr the ruler of Cardigan. The Latin book would have honoured this state of conciliation between the nations and advertised well St Davids' right to grow into a medieval bishopric.

Rhigyfarch himself was a supporter of the traditions of the ancient Celtic Church and so his life includes all manner of fantastic legendary episodes. This is in sharp contrast to the later lives of St David. These were written by members of the Roman Church who removed all the Celtic features of the tales to leave only the bare religious bones. Dewi's character in Rhigyfarch's 'Life' is that of a pious hero with magical saintly powers and it can give us some idea of the spirit of the time even though this version was written six centuries after his actual life. We do not know what sources Rhigyfarch used to write the book but he probably drew on manuscripts and oral tradition alike, reworking them into this coherent medieval tale of Wales' holiest man.

The birth of St David was foreseen by angels thirty years before the event actually occurred. The angels went to see the man who was fated to be his father, Sanctus ruler of Ceredigion, and told him that he must go hunting and give the fruits of his hunt to a monastery. So he went hunting and through Gods blessing he caught a majestic stag, a shining fish and a large beehive. These three gifts were given to him by God because they represented the wisdom, abstinence and strength that would be given by the lord to the unborn child.

The angels soon visited Pembrokeshire a second time when St Patrick had come to Wales from Ireland with the intention of praying to the people. He landed in Ceredigion then went south along the coast to where St Davids stands today. There he was about to preach the Lords' word when a beautiful angel appeared to him. He told Patrick that God had assigned this country to another man who was to be born in thirty years time. The angel also told Patrick not to be troubled or disheartened by this as the lord had chosen Ireland as the place where he should spread the word. So Patrick duly left Wales and the story of his life can be found across the sea in the holy books of Ireland.

After this event thirty years passed until Sanctus Lord of Ceredigion felt compelled to go south to Pembrokeshire. While he travelled there he met an extremely beautiful maiden called Nonita and the king became filled with such desire that he violated her in a meadow. As the woman conceived the earth rejoiced and two stones grew upwards from the ground, one at her head and the other at her feet. These stones were sent both to protect her modesty and to show the importance of the child that had been conceived.

After this she went straight to the church, for it was custom then for people to give alms in church for conceiving a child. As she entered to bless her child the priest who was addressing the congregation was quickly struck dumb and was unable to offer a single word of prayer. All he was able to do was ask his congregation to go outside to give him the chance to pray alone. Nonita became afraid and so hid herself in the corner of the church while the frightened priest tried his best to pray.

He found that he still could not utter a single word in praise of his Lord and in desperation he called out to ask if anyone else was present. Nonita soon revealed herself to the puzzled priest who asked her to go outside while the congregation came back in. When they did this the priest found himself able to pray freely once more and he marvelled at the power the mother possessed. Nonita said that she had only come to bless her unborn child but everyone wondered at the event. They all knew that it was a sign that the child she was carrying would grow into the wisest and most

59

dignified among all the learned men of Britain.

Soon enough the local ruler came to hear of this child who was fated to be known and respected over the whole of the Isle of Britain. He was a selfish man who craved only power and worldly things so he called his magicians and asked them for information about the child. They told him the exact place where the child would be born and so the jealous king decided that he would go to that spot on the day of the birth and kill the wonder child.

Nine months later Nonita was heading for the spot that God had chosen for her to give birth. The lord was travelling there also, eager to find the mother and child. As she arrived at the place Nonita felt the pains of birth come upon her and there at that very spot the heavens opened up with a loud fury of thunder and lightning as rain and hail poured heavily to the ground. This downpour was so forceful that people refused to venture out in it and the lord soon left for home thinking that a woman wandering out on her own would never be able to give birth in such terrible weather.

Nonita was well protected however for when she reached the appointed place and began to give birth the weather became calm all around her and the place shone with a brilliant light even though heavy clouds obscured the sun. While she suffered the immense pains of labour she leaned heavily on a nearby stone for support. The pain was so great that her hands left deep imprints on the stone and it broke in two pieces with sympathy. On this spot a church was later built and the stone still lies concealed in its foundations.

After this the child was born and was baptised Dewi by Ailbe, an Irish bishop from Munster who was travelling in Wales. During the baptism Movi, a blind man, was holding the child under the water when some of the water fell onto his eyes. Immediately he saw light streaming through them and his sight was restored. Where this miracle baptism took place there also appeared a spring of pure water that was used for all the local baptisms after that.

The boy spent his young life in the church learning about the Lord's teachings and the other boys there were surprised to see a dove that taught Dewi and sung hymns to him. Soon enough Dewi was ordained as a priest and went to the holy man Paulinus to be taught by him. He was there many years and during this time Dewi's wisdom increased and he set to his memory all that he read.

60

One day the young lad even cured his teacher Paulinus of blindness. An angel soon appeared to Paulinus to tell him that as Dewi was a man of such grace and wisdom, he must go all around the country to preach to as many people as possible. Dewi did this and was soon teaching the word of God to people in ways they would best understand. Some people he entreated to join the monasteries and there they lived in accordance with God's will but with others he merely warned them away from the sins of materialistic greed. By teaching in this way he affected many lives and soon became all things to all the people he met.

During these travels he founded a church at Glastonbury and then purified the poisoned waters of Bath, making them warm and suitable for bathing once more. Then he went to Crowland, Repton, Colva and Glascwm, and there he founded the monastery of Leominster. Then he went through Raglan in Gwent to the monastery of Llangyfelech. There he cured Proprius, king of Erging, of blindness and then returned to the place where his journey had begun.

An angel then came to him and told him of a place nearby where all the inhabitants had been doomed to Hell. Dewi resolved to save these people and was joined by Aidan, Eliud and Ismael who were three of his best disciples. They all travelled to this place and lit a fire to claim the land for God. The smoke from this fire blew high in the air and such was the faith of the four that it encircled the whole of Britain and Ireland with its protection.

Nearby lived a king called Baia and he saw this smoke while he was on the ramparts of his fort. The fire meant that someone was claiming rights to part of his lands and as the smoke obscured the rays of the sun Baia became sad at the sight of this portent and lost all his appetite. At the end of the day his wife came to him and asked why he had not eaten his food. He replied that the smoke coming from Rosina Vallis had saddened him for it was surely an omen for the growing glory of someone who would have power over men like himself.

His wife, who was a bitter woman, advised him to take some slaves to where the smoke was coming from and attack whoever they found there. The king agreed to this and set out with some of his men but before they even reached Rosina Vallis they were struck by an awful fever. By the time they arrived at the fire the fever had made them too weak even to walk. All they could do was shout taunts and obscenities at Dewi and his disciples from the ground. Baia then turned back for home but his wife met him on the way. She told them that all their cattle had suddenly died and entreated Baia to return and beg the forgiveness of the monks.

Although he did not want to beg to the monks he had no choice but to return to Dewi and beg his forgiveness. Baia went to him and offered him the land he had settled on as a gift to do with as he wished. Dewi replied with kindness and forgave Baia and his wife promising to bring their cattle back to life. Baia and his wife were thankful for this and when they returned to their land they did indeed find their cattle alive again.

Soon after this however Baia's wife became angry at the humiliating treatment they had received from Dewi and the monks. This anger boiled inside her so much that she gathered together all her maids and ordered them to go Rosina Vallis. There, where the monks could see them, they stripped naked and acted lewdly in front of them, playing rude games and imitating love-making in front of the monks. Some of the monks watched this spectacle and became tempted by lust but most were merely irritated by it. The monks soon decided however that they should leave the place because of this aggravation and they entreated Dewi to do this.

Dewi could not agree to leaving and so he told his monks that to achieve anything they must stand fast in the face of adversity. He told them they must not let evil overcome them but must let good prevail. At these words the monks were heartened and gladly ignored the women. When the maids saw that they were having no more effect on the monks they left.

When Baia's wife heard that Dewi had once again thwarted her she went mad and slew Dunawd her step-daughter before disappearing. Baia himself was eventually killed as his enemies caught him by surprise one day and burnt down his fortress. Some say it was because of his attempt on Dewi's life that this misfortune fell upon him.

Dewi was now free to start building a monastery on the site which had been shown to him by an angel. Here all the monks toiled hard through the day, ploughing the soil and growing their own food. They worshipped God daily and devoted their lives to him, scorning the riches and possessions of the world. They did not want for anything and lived a simple life with everything they needed made available to all, each monk had an equal share of food and also completed an equal amount of work.

In the summer the brethren gathered together to complain to Dewi about their water supply. Due to the great heat the nearby river was reduced to a trickle and would not give them the water they needed. After hearing this Dewi went to a quiet place and prayed until a spring broke forth from the earth. One of their neighbours also came to him for he was also without water so Dewi went to his land and, simply by placing his staff on the ground caused a spring to pour forth. It gave cold pure water even in the hottest days of summer and the farmer was very thankful.

One day St Aidan was reading his Bible outside the monastery when Dewi asked him to go to the woods with the oxen to get some timber. Aidan dropped his book on the floor in his hurry to obey his master and went with the oxen along the dangerous cliff side path. He got to the forest easily enough but on his way back the wagon fell into the sea taking the oxen with it. Aidan managed to make the sign of the cross over the animals before they fell and they escaped from the sea unharmed because of this. When he returned to the monastery although it was raining he also found his book safe and dry where he had left it in the field. Thus Aidan protected the oxen for his holy master and Dewi likewise protected the book for his obedient disciple.

St Aidan soon completed his studies and became a good and wise man. He set out for Ireland and founded a monastery there called Guernin. Everything went well until one Easter eve when an angel appeared to him. The angel warned him that Dewi was about to be poisoned by some of his own brethren because of jealousy. He also advised St Aidan to send one of his servants to warn Dewi but Aidan replied that there were no ships ready and the wind was blowing the wrong way for the journey. At this the angel told him to not to worry and to send Scuthinus, one of his servants, down to the beach. Scuthinus went to the beach and there he found a strange but wonderful sea animal waiting for him which took him across the sea on its back. Scuthinus and the creature arrived at the city just as Dewi had finished the Easter service and was walking to the refectory to eat. There Scuthinus told Dewi all that the angel had told St Aidan.

Later they all sat down to eat and the deacon came to Dewi, laying the poisoned bread in front of him. Scuthinus immediately stood up and told the deacon that he would wait on Dewi instead. He broke the bread into three pieces and gave them to Dewi who ordered his brethren to feed one of the thirds to a dog and one to a crow. They did this and each animal died as soon as the bread touched their mouths. Seeing this Dewi blessed his own portion of bread and calmly ate it while the brethren stood amazed, expecting their master to die. They all watched him intently for hours but Dewi's faith was so great that the poison had no effect on him at all.

One day after this an abbot called Barre who had been on a long pilgrimage on the continent decided to return to his monastic life in Ireland. Near the end of his journey he spent a while visiting Dewi. He enjoyed the conversation so much however that he missed the winds that his ship needed to travel across the sea. Soon he became worried for he was sure that because of his long absence his brethren would be arguing amongst themselves and destroying the monastery through needless quarrel. Searching for another way to reach home he eventually came across Dewi's horse in its stable. He went to Dewi and requested from him both the horse and a blessing, which he granted. Then Barre, with his faith and Dewi's blessing, rode the horse down to the quay and out into the sea. The horse did not hesitate for a moment and was soon riding over the waves as if it was travelling across open fields.

While he journeyed to Ireland he met St Brendan riding the opposite way atop a marvellous sea creature. St Brendan marvelled at the sight of Barre coming towards him on a horse and he praised God for the power of the saint's faith. He greeted Barre and when he heard about Dewi he vowed to go and meet with him. After he said his farewells Barre soon reached his monastery where, to his gladness, he found everything in order. The monastery kept Dewi's horse its service and when it died they made a statue of it from gold which gave miraculous blessings to all that visited it.

One day it was time for Dewi himself to travel and an angel came and told him to go to Jerusalem. The angel also told him that St Teilo and St Paternus would meet with him tomorrow and, even though each of them lived three days travel from the other, the next morning they all met together as foretold and set out in a boat across the English Channel. The three men travelled on their long journey as if they were one and they made many new converts on the journey as Dewi, blessed with the gift of languages, was able to preach in strange lands.

When they finally came to Jerusalem the patriarch, who had been told of their arrival by an angel, greeted them. There Dewi was made archbishop by the patriarch and the three went to preach in the lands around Jerusalem to increase the faith. When this was done they decided to return to Britain and the patriarch bestowed upon them gifts of a holy altar, a bell, a gold tunic and a staff. These gifts he promised to send on after for they would be too cumbersome on their travels. The three men returned to their monasteries in Britain where the gifts were duly given to them by angels.

At the time of their return the theories of the Pelagian heresy were rising again like a serpent to threaten the British churches so a synod was held for all the bishops of Britain to attend. There were 118 bishops present as well as a host of priests, abbots, kings, princes and onlookers and the crowd was so large that whoever spoke could not reach everyone's ears. The bishops decided to set a huge heap of their garments at a place called Brevi and announced that whoever could be heard by all the people while standing on the mound would be made archbishop of Britain.

The bishops each stood in turn to proudly preach the faith but their words were constricted and only reached the ears of those closest to them. The bishops all despaired at this for the people were thinking of returning home and leaving the heresy unbeaten. At length Paulinus said that there was a man not present at the synod who was of great countenance, wisdom and faith and had also just been made a bishop in Jerusalem. When the other bishops heard Dewi's name they sent messengers out to bid him to come and preach to the people.

When the messengers found Dewi they pleaded with him to go and said that he was desperately needed. Dewi however knew that he was no better than those who had already tried to speak and so he refused to go with them, believing himself to be of no use to them. By the time the messengers returned with the news the synod was nearly breaking up and so finally they sent the holiest men present, namely Daniel and Dubricius to speak with him again. Dewi received them with great humbleness and ordered a meal to be prepared for them but Daniel and Dubricius refused to eat with him

65

until he promised to accompany them to the synod. Not wishing to offend his friends Dewi agreed to go with them to help the other bishops with his prayers.

While they travelled there they heard a great wailing and Dewi hurried to see where it came from. Daniel and Dubricius told him to ignore the cries and hurry to the synod before everyone left but Dewi only ignored them. He soon found a woman crying over the body of her young son and, when she saw Dewi approaching, she entreated him to help her. Dewi's compassion for the woman was great and he cried over the boy's corpse. His grief miraculously returned warmth and life into his body and after this the woman could not thank him enough and gave her son to Dewi so that he might learn about the life of God.

Dewi entered the synod with the boy on his shoulders and was greeted with great rejoicing. He accepted the crowd's invitation to speak and stood high on the pile of garments where a white dove flew onto his shoulder. He spoke with such a loud clear voice that all those present, near and far could hear his words of wisdom clearly. As he spoke thus the ground beneath him rose into a hill so that all those present could see him while he preached with a voice that travelled as loud and clear as a trumpet. Later on to celebrate this miracle a church was built on the hill.

After he spoke the heresy was expelled by the bishops and Dewi was made archbishop over the entire British race by the consent of all those at the synod. St Davids was also declared the metropolis of the whole country so that whoever was bishop there after Dewi would also be archbishop. Then the bishop Dewi became the wise leader of all men, women and children. If they were weak he gave them strength, if they were needy he provided for them and if they wished instruction he taught it to them. He was all things to all the people and Britain became a holy place filled with hosts of the monks that he tutored.

He led the Christian race of the Britons in this way until he reached a wise age. In that year, eight days before the first of March, an angel came to him. He said to Dewi that the day he had been waiting for was nearly upon him and that he must prepare himself for it. With these words the sky became filled with a bright white light and the air hummed to the sound of melodious voices. Then the angel went to the brethren of the monastery and told them that on the first of March they would be visited by angels who would come to take Dewi to heaven.

At first they lamented greatly at the news but Dewi told them to have strength for they still had their lives left to come. Dewi stayed with his monks and preached for all the days afterwards while angels travelled all over the country to tell the news to the wise and pious people. When the day was nearly upon them there was assembled a great host of holy men and believers from all over Britain and beyond. The whole city flowed with tears with the young weeping as if for their fathers and the old weeping as if for their sons.

On Sunday he preached a wise and uplifting sermon to the assembled host, then he consecrated the bread and wine. Immediately after taking them his illness became worse and he blessed the people, telling them to continue all the teachings he had given them and to continue devoting their lives to God. All those present wept, fasted and prayed for three days until the time came when Dewi died.

On that day the air was filled with the songs of angels and the gentlest of fragrances. The Lord himself came accompanied by the angels to receive Dewi into the kingdom of Heaven. There, for all his good work, his soul was freed from his body and he lived in everlasting life in the company of God. All that was left was for his holy brethren on earth to take his physical body to be buried in a great procession and so he was laid to rest in the grounds of his own monastery.

So Dewi, the patron saint of Wales, could make animals walk on water, bring forth water in a drought and raise the dead. This 'Life' of Pembrokeshire's famous saint is a prime example of how the saints were thought of in the traditions and beliefs of the middle ages. The story starts off with the strange account of Dewi's conception that seems very unacceptable in a religious story as Dewi's birth occurs through the 'defilement' of a maiden. Dewi's life however is a legend and so it makes perfect sense to give him a mythical birth even if the conception is lacking in both love and marriage.

The story of Merlin's birth offers parallels to this story as it is very similar to Dewi's. Merlin's mother, a nun in Dyfed, was visited by something 'in the form of a man' that made her pregnant. The story says that a number of men have been born in this way and so Dewi is another 'wonder-child' like Merlin. Dewi's mother's name of Nonita simply means 'Nun' while his father's name means 'Saint'. The writer of the 'Life', obviously didn't know the real names of his parents and even though he was using the magical 'miracle-birth' tale he tried to keep some semblance of religious piety by calling Dewi's parents 'Nun' and 'Saint'.

However, with ancestry being so important in Celtic society, Dewi could not carry on in high esteem with parents like these and so a fuller family background was needed to give him the status he needed to become Wales' patron saint. This ancestry is found in a number of manuscripts and the most complete comes from a version of the 'Bonedd y Saint', 'The Descent of the Saints'. This gives Dewi's male line as:

"Dewi son of Sant son of Cedig son of Ceredig son of Cunedda Wledig."

The last name given, Cunedda Wledig, is the name of a famous king who came to Wales from North Britain in the 5th century to expel the Irish settlers from north and west Wales. His family are then said to have established the first Welsh kingdoms and in this way Dewi's great-grandfather, Ceredig, settled in west Wales and gave his name to the ancient kingdom of Ceredigion, a name still used as the name of the county above Pembrokeshire. Dewi's father Sant is therefore the fourth king of Ceredigion and this genealogy gave Dewi and the whole see of St David's the greatest honour.

As if that wasn't enough the ancestry of Dewi's mother's side is also given in the same manuscript and this runs as follows:

"Non was the daughter of Anna, the daughter of Uther Pendragon"

The fame of the figure of Uther Pendragon, the father of King Arthur himself, was great indeed and Non's position as Arthur's cousin is even greater as the relationship of the uncle to the niece or nephew was a sacred one in Celtic society. Dewi's legendary ancestry is therefore as honourable as possible with the original founders of Ceredigion on his father's side and the family of King Arthur on his mother's side. This was thought of as a more fitting parentage for Wales' patron saint and it set the background to his great fame.

Unless we believe in the miracles and angelic visions it is hard to find the real Dewi. Trying to look for this 'real' historical St David who lived nearly 1,500 years ago rather than the legendary one is an almost impossible task. None of his actual writings have survived and so his real life and character is forever buried under the many medieval re-writings of his life. The clergy who wrote these lived over five hundred years after his death and were more interested in the power and influence of the church at St Davids than in historical accuracy. In this way Dewi the person was quickly replaced by Dewi the hero who became a character in his own legendary tale.

There are some ways of getting closer to the historical Dewi though because Rhigyfarch's 'Life' is not the earliest record we have about Dewi. At an important early church in Ceredigion called Llanddewi Brefi there is an inscription, now partly lost, which was recorded by an antiquarian in the seventeenth century. The inscription gives the name of someone who was killed during a raid on the church of St David. This inscription dates from the 7th century and it was carved only a century after Dewi's death. The stone was also found in a church not far from where he is said to have lived and so it is good evidence that he was an important historical person who at least formed a very early monastery or church in the area.

Mentions in the earliest literature give us a similar picture to that portrayed in the 'Life'. In Ireland he is mentioned as early as the eighth century alongside other saints and monks who followed a similar monastic life to his. The Breton writer of a saint's life from the ninth century calls Dewi the 'water drinker' in reference to his pious monastic life. His fame also spread early on to England. There was a cult of St David in Glastonbury as early as the ninth century and they were so fond of him that they even claimed to hold some of his relics. Dewi's name also suprisingly turns up in many English place-names of the early middle ages, for example

69

Dewsbury in Yorkshire and Dewsall in Herefordshire.

The most important early Welsh reference to Dewi is the poem Armes Prydein, 'The Prophecy of Britain'. This poem was a call to all the Celtic peoples to rally together and oppose the growing power of the English. The writer says that the Cymry, or Welsh, must call on Dewi to be their leader in battle as through him they will beat the English and 'raise on high the holy standard of Dewi'. This shows, at least in south Wales where the poem was written, that Dewi was considered the greatest of the Welsh saints and the religious leader of the nation as early as 930 AD when the poem was written.

Apart from the medieval tale we do therefore have at least some indications of Dewi's life and how his character was perceived in the first few centuries after his death. We know that at St Davids there was a monastic establishment, or at least a church, as early as the seventh century and that the fame of his frugal and monastic habits soon spread to Ireland. By the ninth century he was being worshipped in English churches and in the tenth he was already celebrated in Wales as their national hero and the leader of their Christian faith. Therefore we can see, albeit dimly, back to the real life of Dewi even though much of the evidence has been lost.

There is plenty of evidence of the fame and importance of the legendary Dewi. The figure of Dewi the patron saint has always been inseparable from the importance of St David's itself as an ecclesiastical centre. In the small town of St Davids is the cathedral, the bishop's palace and a complex of medieval buildings. The earliest of the surviving buildings date to the 12th and 13th centuries when the Normans were developing the site as a bishopric. Rhigyfarch names the site as Rosina Vallis in Latin and Hodnant in the British language but neither of these names are now used.

Mynyw is now the Welsh name for St Davids but it is also called Ty Ddewi, 'Dewi's house', which may be the oldest church name in the county. Although evidence of Dewi's original sixth century clas or monastery no longer survives there are several inscribed stones, some with beautiful intricate designs, which date from the 7th to 10th centuries. These suggest a very early foundation date for settlement here.

The early Welsh Annals have a few early entries that concern the town and church of St Davids. These Annals start around the year

440 AD and consist of a one line description of the year's main event. They first tell of the birth of St David in 458 and go on to record events like the 'Hammering of Dyfed' in 645 when David's monastery was burnt, an event repeated in 810 and 906. Other annal records concern the deaths of the bishops of St Davids, such as Nobis in 840 and Llunferth in 946.

An idea of St David's growing status in medieval times can be seen in the triad of the 'Three Tribal Thrones of Britain'. One of these thrones is named as St David's that has King Arthur as chief prince and Dewi as its bishop. This replaced an earlier version of the same triad which named the royal court of Aberffraw in Gwynedd instead of St Davids. The author of the triad, like Rhigyfarch, was obviously keen to amplify the prestige of St Davids at the cost of the ancient royal seat of Aberffraw.

St Davids was not the first site to be associated with St David. This place, which brings us back to the subject of the real figure of Dewi, is a short distance north-west of St Davids near Whitesands Bay. This is the site of Rosnant, otherwise called Ty Gwyn, which was probably the place where St Patrick stayed when he came over to Wales in the story. The foundation seems to have been started by Irish monks, possibly St Patrick himself, and it was the place where the Irishman Ailbe baptised Dewi. The site is now abandoned and nothing remains of the site apart from a few lumps in the ground, possibly the remains of the wall bases. It could have been abandoned for many reasons, possibly it was not easily defendable or because sand blew into the buildings. The more likely reason is that an increasing amount of sand was filling the bay, making it more and more inaccessible to boats

Although there is little trace of this original settlement, place names are common in the area. On the northern end of Whitesands Bay is Penmaen Dewi, 'David's Head or Rock'. Across the sea from here is Ramsey Island, which is called Ynys Dewi, 'David's Island'. His legendary birthplace is also found to the south of St Davids at the chapel dedicated to his mother St Nons. A few kilometres to the north east of St Davids is Maen Dewi, 'Dewi's Stone', and there are also many wells called Fynnon Dewi dedicated to him in the area as well as a few more Maen Dewis. On the river Alun, which flows past the cathedral, is Pont Cerwyn Dewi, 'The Bridge of Dewi's Vat', the vat being a cauldron shaped hole formed by the river. The

71

whole landscape of the peninsula is riddled with Dewi place-names and it is likely that some of them at least originated during his lifetime or not long after his death.

With St David being such a holy man it is not surprising that there are many churches dedicated to him. In Cemais there is a St Davids Chapel which is near a mound called Cnwc y Dewy where he is said to have prayed. In Narberth is his church of Llandewi Velfrey and further afield there is Llanddewi on the Gower peninsula, Llanddewi Rhydderch in Gwent, Llanddewi Ystradenni in Powys and even Dewchurch in Herefordshire. The occurance of place names such as Llandewi, Capel Dewi and Fynnon Dewi around Wales are a testimony to his fame.

There is one place name that reminds us both of the Irish settlers who lived in the area and Rhigyfarch's story. The place is Clegyr Boia, 'Boia's Rock', a small settlement one kilometre west of St Davids which is named after the Irish king Baia in the legend. Rhigyfarch would have known much about the Irish settlement of Pembrokeshire but it is unclear whether King Baia was an actual historical figure. There is some evidence as the name is known in Ireland among the Deisi tribe, the same tribe that settled in Pembrokeshire, and so there is more than a possibility that the character is based on fact. There is also another piece of evidence just over a kilometre to the south west of Clegyr Boia. Here is a small bay called Porthlysgi which is said to be named after Lisci son of Paucant who, in another version of the life of St David, was named as the king who raided Pembrokeshire and slew Baia. This small bay would have been a perfect place for a raider like Lisci to have landed and attacked Baia. These place-names either show the effect the tale of Dewi and its characters had on the landscape or they are remnants of real events forever remembered in the features of Pembrokeshire.

Other contacts Pembrokeshire had with Ireland feature prominently in the story. Porth Mawr or Whitesands Bay near St Davids was the perfect stopover point for travellers coming over from Ireland. The number of monks who travel between Wales and Ireland in the story show clearly how close the links were between the Irish and Welsh Celtic church. The interesting detail in our story of how St Patrick came over but was turned back by the advice of angels was probably created to give the Welsh church sole

72

claim to the area. The Irish church was very powerful at this time and so the myth came to strengthen the independence of St Davids.

As well as the many place-names there are also various pieces of folklore about Dewi and St Davids to be found in Pembrokeshire. One of the stories is that while Dewi was praying one night he was interrupted by the sweet melodies of the nightingale. He could not fix his mind on his meditations because of the bird so he prayed to the Lord to rid him of it. So it is said from that time to this no nightingale is ever heard in the whole of the diocese of St David's as a result of his prayer. Two other stories will be given later on in the book. One is about a magical bridge over the River Alun at St Davids that was called Llech Lafar, 'The Speaking Stone'. The other is about how the fairy islands could be seen out to sea if you took a turf from St Davids and stood on it on the coast.

The death of the great St David probably happened around 588 or 589 AD and his birth probably occurred around 520 AD, giving him the respectable age of nearly 70. He is said to have died on the 1st March, which gives us St David's Day, and the observation of this day still carries on in Wales with the wearing of leeks or daffodils and the holding of meals in his honour. As this is celebrated over 1400 years after his death it is quite a tribute to the saint and the strength of the national identity that he stands for.

We have seen how the ancient figure of St David, like other culture heroes, acted like a magnet to attract legends, place-names, church dedications and folklore until the real Dewi was obscured and lost beneath the heroic and miraculous patron saint. It is very unfortunate, because of the timescale involved, we don't have an adequate record of his life. What Dewi and his fellow saints actually achieved in the tempestuous period of the dark ages must have been very special indeed. The story of St David is a vivid testimony to the spirit of all the early saints who peacefully converted the Welsh to Christianity and at the time advanced Wales' culture and spiritual unity.

# St Teilo

Although St David is the most famous of the Welsh saints there is a whole host of others from the sixth century. We have already briefly met St Teilo in the last story as one of Dewi's fellow pilgrims to Jerusalem. St Teilo, like Dewi, was a widely known Welsh saint and in an ancient triad he is named alongside Dewi and Padarn as one of the 'Three Blessed Visitors of the Island of Britain'. He was born at Eccluis Cunian, now called Penally near Tenby, and he turned to religion at an early age. He was taught by the great Paulinus and spent his early years as a pupil alongside Dewi at the monastery of Ty Gwyn at Whitesands Bay.

His 'Life' is found in the Book of Llandaf and just as Dewi's 'Life' was written to raise the status of the bishopric of St Davids, so St Teilo's was published to increase the influence and claims of the see of Llandaf in Glamorgan. Teilo was claimed as Llandaf's first bishop and founder but earlier traditions found in the Book of St Chad indicate that this was not the case and that his original monastery was at Llandeilo Fawr in Carmarthenshire. Eventually it seems that due to the proximity of St Davids and the attraction of the growing church at Llandaf all the traditions of his life were moved eastwards to Glamorgan.

It is because of this that he is mainly associated with Carmarthenshire and Glamorgan. Although he was known all over Wales and there is a lot of evidence that shows he spent a large part of his life in Pembrokeshire. There are twelve churches within the diocese of St David's alone that claim to have been founded by him and a legend from one of these churches at Llandeilo Llwydarth shows that St Teilo left a permanent impression on the religious life of Pembrokeshire. Llandeilo Llwydarth is an old church near Maenclochog and although there is little remaining of the medieval church itself, three early inscribed Christian stones were found there. These stones are dated to the 5th and 6th century AD and they indicate that the religious site was founded in the dark ages. The stones are also unique in that they commemorate three members of the same family.

The circular 'clas' enclosure of Llandeilo Llwydarth church, which is marked by a stone wall, is another archaeological feature of an early Christian site as is St Teilo's well which stands about

100 metres to the north-east of the ruined church. The well, which is made of crude stone, was famed for healing respiratory diseases like tuberculosis and whooping cough and it has probably been venerated for its healing powers for thousands of years. Gaining the benefits of this water was not a simple practice though because the well's water was only effective if it was drunk from Penglog Teilo, a piece of St Teilo's skull.

This tradition of drinking from the skull was observed by visiting pilgrims at the beginning of this century. The healing powers of the well were considered useless if the skull was not used and last century it was looked after by the Melion family who lived in the nearby farmhouse of Llandeilo. During 1914-18 many visitors used the skull and the well to ask for an end to the Great War and the safe return of their relatives. The custom is not unique for across Britain and Ireland there are similar holy wells that used sacred skulls as drinking implements such as Ffynnon Llandyfaen in Carmarthenshire. In medieval times holy relics of saints such as skulls became an important feature of Christian worship. These beliefs were so strong that a medieval bishop of St Davids once had to destroy some silver-encased skulls that were being kept in the church as relics. The beginnings of this tradition probably lie in pagan times when the skull linked the spirit of the sacred ancestor with the healing deity of the well. It is highly improbable that the skull itself, which was the remains of a brain pan, was genuinely St Teilo's but legends still grew around the belief.

There are two other legends about the body of St Teilo, one of which is connected to Llandeilo Llwydarth and the he first of these begins right after his death. Three churches were arguing over the right to bury his body because of the fame and popularity it would bring to their foundations. Priests from the churches at Llandaff, Llandeilo Fawr and Penally all claimed the body and there seemed no way of resolving the problem as all of these churches had a good argument for having the body. St Teilo had been bishop at Llandaf, had died at Llandeilo Fawr and was born at Penally where his family was also buried. Eventually the eldest priest gave up and decided to let God choose the right one. He told the others to go to bed and when they awoke in the morning the wondrous sight of three bodies, all exactly the same, confronted them. They thanked the Lord for his ingenuity and each priest took one of the corpses to

75

bury in their respective churches.

This legend is a useful way of explaining how three churches in south Wales all claimed to hold the body of St Teilo, but unfortunately Llandeilo Llwydarth is not one of these churches and so it never even received a body. The story of how the sacred skull came to Llandeilo Llwydarth is given in a second legend about St Teilo's body. These stories are fine examples of how legends were once living things crafted and altered to serve the needs of the real world.

The story goes that St Teilo was lying on his death bed around the year 566 AD and was fortunate to be attended by a maid servant from Llandeilo Llwydarth. Just before he breathed his final breath he told her to swear that exactly a year after his burial at Llandeilo Fawr in Carmarthenshire she would take his skull and place it at the nearby well. St Teilo asked her to do this so that the local people could benefit from the holy waters and be cured of their ailments by his holy relic. A year later she honoured her promise and carried out his request bringing the holy skull to Llandeilo Llwydarth. It is a fine testimony to the power of tradition that the well and its skull still survived as a place of worship long after the nearby church of Teilo was in ruins and forgotten.

## St Patrick & Ireland

Although St Patrick was turned back by an angel when he came to Wales he had as much of success in Ireland as Dewi did in Wales, becoming the patron saint of the country. Also, just as we find Dewi's name in early Irish monastic manuscripts so we find Patrick's name in the landscape of Pembrokeshire. The medieval southern gate of St Davids Close was called Porth Padrig, 'Patrick's Gate', there is a Llanpadrig in Pembroke Dock and there was also a now lost 'Capel Padrig' in Cemais.

The other place-name evidence points to similar traditions to those in the Life of St David. The life mentions an Eisteddfa Padrig, 'Patrick's Seat' from where the saint was shown the country of Ireland by God after being warned off Wales by the angel. Although the site of this is now unknown there is still a Carn Padrig, 'Patrick's Rock', on the west coast of the peninsula of St Davids. It is sited on the sea routes in an area where travellers from

Ireland would disembark and this gives Carn Padrig a good reason to be associated with a legend or an actual visit from the great Irish saint.

Not far from Carn Padrig is another indication of the saint's influence, namely a chapel dedicated to St Patrick. This chapel was probably abandoned before the 15th century and all that remains today are the lowest remnants of the walls and the foundations lying in a coastal field at Porth Mawr, or Whitesand Bay. The chapel was excavated in 1924 to reveal a simple rectangular building made of dry stone boulders with an altar built at one end. In the chapel was the skeleton of a young man was buried in front of the altar and another skeleton was buried by the wall opposite the altar. The chapel was built on top of some other human remains which indicates an earlier Christian or pagan burial place. Burials are frequently found in early Irish chapels and at St Justinian's chapel only two kilometres to the south two skeletons were found inside the walls.

Although nothing found in the excavation could be dated there is no evidence to suggest that the chapel did not belong to the age of the saints. It is sited perfectly on a bay where many Irish travellers would have disembarked from their ships, using the chapel to offer thanks for the safe journeys they had made. The chapel presumably lost its passing flock when the bay became silted up and unsuitable for ships. It is worth noting that an episode in one Life of Dewi tells of how St David raised an old priest called Criumther from the dead while he was at Porth Mawr waiting to go to Ireland. This must have taken place at or around the Irish chapel of St Patrick and perhaps Criumther's body at one time lay alongside the other skeletons found in the chapel.

## St Brynach

The close contacts that existed between the religious movements in Ireland and Wales feature heavily in the life of St Brynach. He was known as Brynach Wyddel, 'Brynach the Irishman', and was married to one of the daughters of King Brychan. This king was the ruler and founder of Brycheinog, the modern county of Brecknock in Powys. King Brychan also came from Ireland and he is credited with having ten sons and twenty-four daughters, most of whom became saints. The family's fame spread far and wide over Wales. Caer Farchal in Dewsland is dedicated to Saint Marchell the mother of Brychan. Clydai church is also meant to have been named after Clydai, one of Brychan's many daughters.

The 'Life' of St Brynach is found in a Latin manuscript that dates from the twelfth century. The same manuscript also includes the lives of other eminent Welsh saints such as Cadoc and Illtud. Brynach the Irishman came over from Ireland and must have spent most of his life in north east Pembrokeshire. The churches at Dinas, Nevern, Llanfrynach, Pontfaen and Henrysmoat which are dedicated to him, show that he had a great influence in the area. There is also a Ffynnon Brynach near Maenclochog that had a well chapel associated with it, and a healing well dedicated to him at the church of Llanfrynach in Nevern. The latter well is within a stone enclosure called Buarth Brynach, 'Brynach's Enclosure' and there are also four other Ffynnons and Pistyll Brynachs in north Pembrokeshire.

The story of St Brynach's life gives us some of the story behind these bare place-names. St Brynach had been preaching in Brittany and he stood on the coast of Armorica and wished he was in Wales. He went down to the sea shore and put a stone on the water and it floated him over the sea to Milford Haven. Here he settled and married Corth, one of the daughters of Brychan Brycheiniog and he was given lands in Emlyn. His wife was somehow not happy with this arrangement and she soon became bitter and sent men to murder Brynach. One of these man stabbed Brynach with his lance but a swarm of winged ants came to protect the saint and they stung the man to death. Brynach then went to bathe his wound in a nearby spring and this became known as Ffynnon Goch, 'Red Well', which is probably the Ffynnon Coch in Llanfair-Nantgwyn parish in Cemais.

The saint then travelled to the river Caman. An angel had previously told him that a wild white boar and her litter would come to him by the river and show him the site for his monastery. When he arrived there he lit a fire to claim his right to the land just as Dewi had done. The local lord came to see who dared light a fire in his lands. Unlike Baia however this king was kind-hearted and he gave the land to the saint without any trouble and also promised to send his sons to be educated by Brynach. After this the white boar appeared and led him to the foot of Carn Ingli mountain, which is said to be named after the angels who frequently appeared to Brynach. Here he built his monastery and when it was complete it is said that St David visited him there on his way to Llandewi Brefi church in Ceredigion.

There is a curious tale about an inscribed stone known as St Brynach's stone at St Brynach church in Nevern. In the churchyard a cuckoo used to sing every year on the 7th April, or St Brynach's day, and the parish priest would not start mass until the cuckoo came and sang. The bird usually perched on top of St Brynach's stone, which stood in the church yard, but one day the bird came to the stone and fell dead before singing a note. No reason is given why this strange thing happened or if the mass continued as usual. The stone was said to have been given to St Brynach by St David himself when he visited the church. The decorated medieval cross at Nevern is probably meant to be the stone in the legend but it was probably a much simpler cross, many examples of which are housed at Nevern church.

## St Gofan

It seems that the holy St Gofan spent most of his religious life as a recluse at the southernmost tip of Pembrokeshire. St Govan's Head is a unique and important early Celtic Christian site for, dramatically sited on a fissure in the sea cliffs, is a chapel and well dedicated to St Gofan. This chapel can only be reached from the cliff top by a flight of stone steps which are impossible to count according to tradition. The chapel building itself is set into a cleft in the cliff. Inside there is an altar and a stone bench which encircles most of the walls and the building itself dates from the 13th or 14th century. As St Gofan lived in the sixth century an earlier chapel probably existed on the site which would have been obliterated by the later buildings.

Before the steps were carved in the cliff the position of this chapel would have offered the exact environment of solitude and contemplation that an early ascetic like Gofan would have been looking for. His well is found among some loose rocks further down the cliff and the existence of this important water source may have been his reason for choosing this site. The well can now only be reached by walking through the chapel itself and it is famed for its healing properties, especially for bad eyesight and crippled limbs. This holy water was said to be so effective that some people who came on crutches walked away freely without them, which would be quite a task considering the hard walk up to the cliff-top. The well was last used for healing in the mid nineteenth century but is now unfortunately dry as its water source has disappeared.

The cleft in the rock near the chapel is traditionally said to be able to neatly fit a person whatever their size. This magical fissure is said to have been used by St Gofan when he was being pursued by some angry pagans. While he ran he came across some farmers in a nearby field who were sowing barley and he told them to fetch their reaping hooks. He also told them that if anyone came along asking after him they were to answer that they had seen him pass while they were sowing their crops. He then went to hide in the cleft and when the man returned with their reaping hooks they were amazed to see the barley they had been planting moments before was fully grown and ready for reaping. Gofan's pursuers soon came along asking for the saint and the farmers swiftly answered that they had seen him in sowing time. The pursuers, seeing the fields of swaying ripe barley, saw that he was long gone and so gave up the chase.

The magical cleft where Gofan hid, which is said to contain the impression of a human figure, was also meant to have been the hiding place for Sir Gawain as he hid from some other pagan pursuers. Here though it seems that St Gofan has been confused with Gawain the Arthurian knight and it seems more likely that it was St Gofan who originally hid from 'pagan persecutors'. This legendary tale probably has an element of truth in it as Gofan probably chose this solitary site because it was hidden from the general population and offered safety in its anonymity. The site is also unique because it has not been built upon or developed and so it retains the same atmosphere and setting as it would have when Gofan himself was alive.

## Female Saints

So far we have only been discussing the prominent male saints but female saints were also numerous during the age of saints in

Wales. There seems to have been much more sexual equality in the early church than in the middle ages. This may be because the early church followed on from pagan traditions where the feminine aspects were worshipped by society and not just pushed to one side. Many of the female saints are now forgotten but it is fortunate that there are some placenames that include the names of saints and martyrs that we would otherwise know nothing about. Examples of this are Capel Gwendith, named after Gwendydd, Llanstadwell named after Ystradfael, and a Ffynnon Ddwysant, or 'Well of the Two Female Saints', in Cilgerran.

It was the passing of the ages that forgot these once renowned women in favour of the male figures. Now the only stories that survived the test of time are about women who are associated with famous men. It is folk tradition rather than the written lives that gives us a better picture of the influences of these women. The ritual site dedicated to her overlooks St Non's bay and includes St Non's chapel, St Non's well and the 7th century inscribed stone known as St Non's Cross. There is also a family connection nearby as the church of Llanwnwr in Dewsland is possibly dedicated to her father Gwynnwr. St Non's early Christian site is at the centre of an important ritual landscape dedicated to St Non and the birth of Dewi.

Another well known female saint in Pembrokeshire is St Canna. All we hear about her from the Latin lives are the names of her husbands and children. She marries a St Sadwrn, gives birth to a St Crallo and after Sadwrns death she marries an Alltu Redegog and gives birth to St Elian Geimiad. She also apparently accompanied St Cadfan as he brought some settlers from Brittany to Britain but apart from this the old books are silent. Traditionally she is associated with the very east of Pembrokeshire near Llandewi-Velfrey. Here the church of Llangan is dedicated to her but more importantly there is a holy well that was famed for its curing of ailments, especially intestinal complaints. The sick person would throw a bent pin in the well, then drink or bathe with the water. Finally they would go to the north east of the church to sit on a large rock called Canna's chair. The rock has a hollow depression in it like a seat which was said to have been formed from the many visits of the sick and it helped the healing process immensely if the ill person managed to fall asleep on the stone.

81

The rock itself is undateable and has the word 'Canu' inscribed on it above the depression. Although it cannot be proved the rock was probably an integral part of Canna's sacred healing site from very early on. The folklore and tradition about the chair and well also show us that this area was probably Canna's main sphere of influence and that she was strongly associated with the healing powers of the sacred well. Even if these traditions began later than her real life it still tells us more about her qualities and attributes than the medieval Latin texts which only tell us who she married and gave birth to.

There is one female saint who left her mark throughout Northern Europe as well as in Pembrokeshire. She is St Brighid, or St Bride, the patroness of Ireland and there are more churches dedicated to her in Britain and Ireland than there are to any other saint. Her fame is hardly surprising when we consider that Brighid was originally a Celtic goddess associated with light and purity. Her Christian festival of the 1st February is also the Celtic festival of the beginning of spring and so she represented this period's new life and creative energy.

Traces of her worship, whether Christian, pagan or both, can be found in Pembrokeshire and the largest bay in the county is named St Bride's Bay after her. Near the coast of this bay in Roose there is a Sain Ffred that was originally Llansanffraid which translates as St Bride's Church. Her birth is entered in the Welsh Annals for the year 454 and this makes her older than St David. Given the close contacts between Wales and Ireland, she is possibly one of the earliest Christian influences in Pembrokeshire, showing that the female saints in this period were as active as their male counterparts.

## Island Settlements

Islands were very popular with the early Christian settlers throughout Britain and isles like Iona and Lindisfarne became important religious centres in the dark ages. Around the coast of Pembrokeshire there are many islands that were suitable for the saints. These islands were often chosen for their solitude as the surrounding sea acted as a barrier from mainland society. The small island of Monkstone is a good example of this and it probably got

its name from an early saint who once lived there but who has left no trace. The importance of larger islands like Ramsey, which is named in Welsh both after the famous Dewi and an unknown Tyfanog, is hard to establish because of the lack of early settlement evidence. There is a small piece of evidence on Ramsey as one of the stones of the island is named Trwynmynachdy, 'The Point of the Abbey'.

Later settlement has often obliterated the traces of these scant settlements. A good example of this is the fort built on St Catherine's Rock which obliterated a small chapel dedicated to St Catherine which stood on its summit. In Ireland Sceilg Mhichíl island provides a good example of an untouched island monastery that was chosen for its solitude. Here on a rocky island in the Atlantic ocean are the remains of early beehive huts, oratories, inscribed stones and a graveyard all dating to the age of the saints.

Apart from their solitude these islands were also the first port of call for the travelling Christian monks. They were ideally situated as they were on the fringe of mainland society but also on the main routes of communication. Ireland, Scotland, Wales, Cornwall and Brittany were all in constant contact through the Irish Sea, Bristol Channel and English Channel. People, products and ideas therefore travelled easily this way and so these island settlements could offer complete solitude for the devotional and also effective contact with the rest of the Christian world.

## Caldey Island

Caldey is a well known island over two kilometres long which lies off the coast of south-east Pembrokeshire near Tenby. The Welsh name for Caldey Island is Ynys Byr or 'Pyr's Island', and not far from here on the mainland is Manorbier which in Welsh is Maenorbyr or 'Pyr's Manor'. These place names show that Pyr was an important person in the area and we are fortunate in this case to have written records about him. The early monastic settlement on Caldey Island is mentioned in the 'Life of St Samson' which names the abbot of the island as Pyro, 'an illustrious and holy priest'.

This life tells us that St Samson went to the monastery to begin his holy and industrious life but while he was there his father fell ill. He left the island to see his father and while he was there he converted both his father and uncle to God, before returning with them to Ynys Pyr. There they met up with the great teacher Dubricius who was staying there for Lent. Dubricius, or St Dyfrig as he is known in Wales, appointed Samson as the steward of the monastery. The existing abbot Pyro was upset at this decision and accused Samson of wasting the island's honey, a charge that was proven to be unfounded. Poor Pyro must have been very unhappy at St Dyfrig's judgements for one night he got blind drunk and while walking around the island in this inebriated state he managed to fall into a well near the monastery. He cried for help and was rescued but shortly afterwards he died from his wounds. The honey he accused Samson of wasting was obviously the main ingredient that he needed for his precious mead.

After this incident St Samson reformed the monastery, causing tension between him and the monks who probably saw Samson as a harsh abbot after being led by Pyro. Samson did not stay there for long however for when some Irish monks visited the island Samson went with them to Ireland and left his uncle in charge of the monastery. When he later returned he saw that his uncle had made a lot of progress on Caldey Island. Samson must have felt that he had done his duties for he refused to run the monastery after that. He went with some companions to Stackpole, also on the south east coast of Pembrokeshire and settled in an ancient camp there. He was soon called again to do the work of God and he ended his days setting up a monastery in Brittany and becoming its first bishop. Samson also appears in Pembrokeshire tradition as a rock-throwing giant but this aspect will be mentioned in a later chapter.

St Samson is portrayed in the story as a righteous and just man and the account of Pyro's demise seems pathetic in comparison with the lavish account of Dewi's death. The story of Pyro is however probably much closer to the truth than the highly embellished account of Dewi's death. This is because the accounts of the ancient saints were rewritten and romanticised by later medieval writers who wanted to increase the fame of their founder fathers. Although the story has been played with to increase the piety of Samson and his right to run the monastery Pyro's death shows how human and vulnerable these early Christians were and incidents like these brings us closer to the actual history of these changing times. St Samson now serves as the patron saint of Caldey Island and the

Cistercian abbey there is also dedicated to him. The abbey's association with St Samson is so strong that in 1919 the Cistercian monks of the isle, who are now celebrating the 900th anniversary of their order, even received some of his holy relics from another church. The memory of poor Pyro is also not forgotten as the Welsh still call the island Ynys Byr after him rather than St Samson.

Possibly the earliest reference to the Christian settlement of the island comes from 'The Life of St Illtyd'. This names an island called Llan Illtyd, where monks from Llantwit Major in Glamorgan formed a colony. It is not certain though that Llan Illtyd was the same place as Caldey Island and any archaeological remains of this dark age settlement probably lie under the medieval monastery which is now in ruins. Of the early community of Pyr and Samson only two pieces of physical evidence remain on the island. At the village church of St Davids the north wall of the sanctuary is thought to be of sixth century origin. There is also an inscribed stone with two inscriptions, one in Irish Ogham script and one in Latin. The earlier Ogham inscription, which dates from the fifth or sixth century, gives the Celtic name of one 'Maglia-Dubracunas' who is unknown, although some have said the name means Dubricious, the Latin form of St Dyfrig.

The stone's Latin inscription, which was probably added later in the ninth century, gives us more information and asks people to pray for the soul of a Catuoconus who himself inscribed two crosses that are on the other side of the stone. This second inscription gives us more important archaeological evidence and confirms that there was Christian activity on Caldey in the ninth century. It is a shame that because the evidence for this whole period is so meagre the few names we have on stone inscriptions rarely match the names we have from the written sources. New discoveries are made all the time though and there may still be more undiscovered stones waiting to be found on Caldey.

## Gateholm Island

Although Gateholm is now a tidal island in medieval times it may have been attached to the mainland. In the age of saints it would almost definitely have been a promontory of the mainland. Although it therefore does not completely belong in this section it proves a useful parallel because unlike Caldey Island there is no written evidence at all about the early settlement of Gateholm. Instead there is a lot of archaeological evidence which has survived partly because there was nothing built later on to destroy it. At the north end of the island is an entrance through a wall that must have defended the land side of the island. It leads to a series of buildings that are either set out in lines along a trackway or neatly arranged around yards.

Parts of the island have been excavated and the buildings were found to have had walls made of a turf and dry stone walling construction. One larger building had two opposing doorways made from upright stone slabs, pits in the centre that may have held roof-poles, and a central hearth. The finds were dated from the third to the thirteenth century but the main period in which the buildings were used seems to be the sixth to the ninth centuries, the right period for Christian settlement. Evidence of settlements from this period in Dyfed is very rare so Gateholm is of the greatest interest to the dark age history of Pembrokeshire. The layout of the large site seems to indicate quite a high level of organisation of the numerous huts. Although it cannot be proved without further excavation that the site was built for a monastic community, it is not improbable that a religious community like that on Caldey Island once lived here. Caldey Island is a good example of a settlement that has plenty of physical evidence but no legends or place-names to give the story of the walls of rock.

## Holy Wells

The practice of using the water that emerged from springs and wells for healing goes back well into prehistoric times. Water, in the form of rivers, springs, wells and lakes had a sacred power in the cultures of many of the Celtic peoples, often involving healing and protection. Archaeologists have found carvings of limbs that were deposited in the sources of rivers in the Iron Age, presumably offered to heal the real limb. Springs, like the famous site at Bath, were also considered blessed with powers of healing, as were certain sacred lakes and pools. Wells, where the water emerged from deep within the earth, were an abundant source for these sacred healing waters. When the early Christians first came to

87

Britain these wells would have often been used in pagan rituals. After the population had been converted these wells were dedicated to the saints but the rituals that took place did not cease, only altering to accommodate the new religious beliefs.

The sheer number of holy wells in Pembrokeshire as compared to the rest of Wales is surprising and shows how important they were to religious worship in the area. There are over 230 holy wells in Pembrokeshire compared with 128 in Carmarthenshire and only 35 in Anglesey and 65 in Monmouthshire. These wells vary greatly in both their traditions and their structure. The well could be a muddy hole in the ground or it could have a stone chapel built over it. Likewise the site could be unknown and known simply as Y Ffynnon, 'The Well', or it could have fantastic legends told about it.

Some of Pembrokeshire's wells are very ancient indeed and are associated with megaliths and other ancient stones. Ffynnon Fair, or 'Mary's Well', stood near a stone at Maenclochog. If this stone was struck it would ring until water from the well was taken into the nearby church. There is also a cromlech near Druid's Well, Canna's stone chair which stood by her well, the now lost Maen Dewi which stood near Ffynnon Dewi near Fishguard and the Mesur y Dorth stone which stood near a well at Penarthur. The association of wells with megalithic, bronze age, and inscribed stones is widespread throughout Europe. The association of the deep well and the tall stone must have once held some deep ritual symbolism.

These ancient pagan well traditions soon gave way to Christianity and hardly a saint in Pembrokeshire lacks a dedicated well. It is hardly surprising therefore to find that so many of these Pembrokeshire wells are dedicated to St David. These wells were formed in many miraculous ways. Dewi created Ffynnon Ddewi in Brawdy by banging his staff on the ground, Pistyll Dewi appeared because of his prayers and his tears falling on the ground caused another Ffynnon Ddewi in Brawdy. Other saints could make water come from the earth in even more spectacular ways. St Decuman's well in South Pembrokeshire sprang up when St Decuman placed his severed head on the ground after carrying it over the channel from Somerset!

Apart from featuring in wonder tales such as these the saint's holy well was also very important in the religious practice of the local communities and, in some instances, the well was more important than the church itself. The wells dedicated to St Govan and St Teilo formed an important part of a ritual site as each is attached to the saint's church or chapel. The chapel and well of both St Non and St Canna are also examples where the use of a saint's well coincided with a service or pilgrimage to the chapel. St Non's well now has a stone vault over it and offerings of gifts, or pins (and pebbles if you were poor) were made to its waters, especially on 2nd March which is St Non's day. A folklorist at the start of this century also wrote that an old man of the area believed that St David himself had been baptised in the well. Another writer said that he was often dipped into the well as a child as the water was particularly useful for protecting children. The power of belief in St Non's well meant that it was used long after the associated chapel was in ruins, just like St Teilo's well at Llandeilo Llwydarth.

There is a story attached to a healing well dedicated to St Edren which once stood halfway between Haverfordwest and Fishguard. The well was in a churchyard and one Sunday a woman dared to wash her clothes in it. She therefore broke the holy law of not working on the Sabbath and thus caused the well to dry up. The waters of the well were very famous for their ability to cure ailments and luckily its healing properties were not lost. After the well had dried they became transferred to the grass of the churchyard and the grass, when eaten with food, had the same healing effect as the well's water.

Different wells were credited with different healing powers. The well at Llanllawer, which dates from the 13th century, was especially effective against sore eyes and St Degfels well in St Dogmaels was good for warts. At Pistyll Meugan there were said to be three streams of water that never mixed. One of the streams was good for the eyes, another for bad joints and the last for the heart.

The rituals that took place at these healing wells were almost as numerous as the wells themselves. The use of St Teilo's skull is an obvious example and there were also rituals of leaving offerings or dropping bent pins into the wells. One old man in 1878 remembered seeing St Canna's well full of pins and the well of Carncwn at Carn Ingli would cure one wart for each pin dropped into it. The Llanllawer well cured sore eyes when pins and coins were offered to it and curses could be made effective if bent pins were offered to it. Bent pins were not always used in this way though as they were offered at Moelgrove well in Nevern without any evil intent.

As well as their creation stories and healing rituals there are also other traditions about holy wells. Letterstone well, near Fishguard, must have been particularly popular. This well was called Ffynnon Shan Shillin as the water was so sought after that it sold for a shilling a bottle. St Caradog's well was the meeting place for lovers and fairs were traditionally held both at Ffynnon Curig and Pistyll Meugan. Gerald of Wales tells us of a man from Cemais who dreamt for three nights of finding a gold necklace under a stone above the waters of a spring. On the third day he went to this well and put his hand under the stone. A viper bit his finger and he died, showing, said Gerald, that dreams should not always be believed. These interesting traditions and rituals make it easy to forget that wells were there primarily for the simple act of procuring water!

Although most wells were once very important religious symbols most of the traditions that took place around them have now died out. Many wells have been forgotten or destroyed or are drying up and becoming blocked through neglect. Thankfully they are now being considered as an important part of the Welsh past. A good example of this changing attitude can be found at Higgin's well at Haverfordwest. It was thought to have been destroyed in the eighteenth century but was rediscovered recently. The bushes that covered it also hid the remains of a well chapel and now it has been repaired, a sign of the care with which we now give to the remnants of our past.

Some of the wells have however continued to be used religiously even into modern times. Although the chapel of St Non's was in complete ruin by the early nineteenth century the nearby St Non's well was restored and re-dedicated by the Roman Catholic Church in 1951 and a pilgrimage was made there. This is a testimony to the enduring power of these special sacred sites whose healing powers were thought to originate from the holiness of the early saints. When we consider the earlier pagan usage of wells some of them have been the focus of religious worship for many thousands of years.

Many of the churches, wells and inscribed stones mentioned in this chapter can be visited by the public and many of them are worth the visit as any tourist guide will show. At a few of the churches it is quite easy to imagine the scene of the small lonely chapel built by the early saint amidst the rolling countryside. Menter Preseli, a group in North Pembrokeshire, has set up trails that take the traveller past many of the best religious sites in the area. Two of these trails lead from Llanwnda and Pontfaen church to St Davids and the latter trail is now being extended through the Preseli mountains to Llanfrynach. These pilgrimage routes are an ideal way to experience a taste of the ancient religious lives of the Celtic saints of Pembrokeshire.

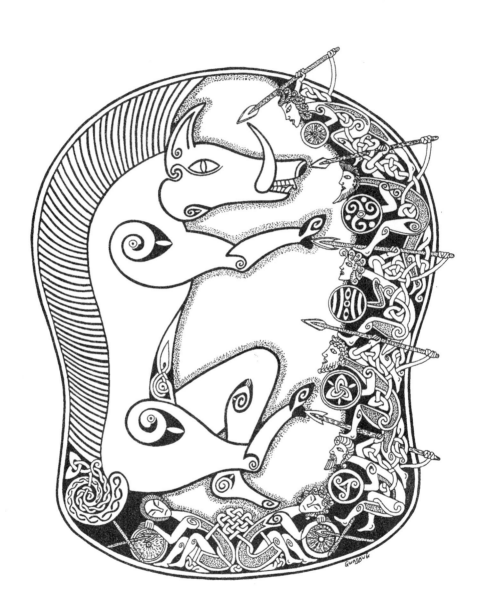

# Chapter Three

## The Legends

So far we have dealt with the legends of the Mabinogion and the saints lives but now it is time to look at a variety of other stories on subjects as diverse as King Arthur, talking stones and killer frogs. These legends and folktales are strange and wonderful stories that deal with all sorts of bizarre and magical themes. They have entertained people for countless centuries, amazing, delighting and bringing smiles to the faces of their audience. As well as this they also told the history of the land and the people and created a solid sense of belonging and unity between people and their landscape because of their real geographical settings.

In the minds of the storytellers the wonders of the Otherworld often mixed freely with the real world to produce fantastic stories. In the first legend, the hunt for the giant boar Twrch Trwyth, these two worlds are used alongside each other to great effect. When the fierce animal goes on the rampage, he does so not in far off mythical lands but through the very real hills and fields of Pembrokeshire. Arthur and his warriors who hunted the boar were also thought of as real people who once trod the ground of Pembrokeshire. In this way giants, monsters and magical stones have all left their impressions in the landscape.

## The Great Boar Hunt

Boars, although now unknown in the wild in Britain, were once a common inhabitant of the great forests that covered the countryside. The boar was the lion of the forest, fierce, savage and deadly. It was such a vicious animal that medieval knights hunted it on horseback protected by full armour and armed with a long boar spear. In Celtic mythology it was a sacred animal that led mortal warriors into the Otherworld. Hunting the animal was a very dangerous task for only the strongest and bravest but a successful hunt brought the rewards of honour and a portion of its highly prized flesh.

The Twrch Trwyth was a legendary boar of gigantic proportions and out of all the magical animals in Welsh legend it was by far the most ferocious. The tale of the hunt of the boar is found together with the Mabinogi legends in the White Book of Rhydderch and the Red Book of Hergest. The story itself forms part of the legend of 'Culhwch and Olwen'. This story is about the warrior Culhwch who seeks the hand of the maiden Olwen. Olwen's father, a fierce giant called Ysbaddaden, hinders their plans for marriage. When Culhwch asks for Olwen's hand in marriage Ysbaddaden sets him many impossible tasks that he must complete before he will give up his daughter. For one of these tasks Ysbaddaden tells Culhwch that he must get some very special objects:

Throughout the world there is not a comb or scissors with which I can arrange my hair, on account of its rankness, except the comb and scissors that are between the two ears of Twrch Trwyth, the son of Prince Tared. He will not give them of his own free will, and thou wilt not be able to compel him.'

*The Mabinogion,* Lady Charlotte Guest

He also names many other rare objects that Culhwch must find before he can even start hunting the boar. The boar's strength is so great that Culhwch must enlist the help of special horses, dogs and huntsmen for the hunt. Culhwch, helped by his uncle King Arthur and many other fine heroes manages to find all the items he needs and so the hunt begins. The quest starts in Ireland where Arthur and a great band of warriors first attack Twrch Trwyth and his seven piglets. The piglets, like Llwydawg Gofynnyad and Grugyn Silver Bristle, are as fierce as their father is and they meet with little success. Even the great Arthur, who fights with them for nine days and nights, can only kill one piglet. After this attack Twrch Trwyth promises to lay waste Arthur's country and sets out for Wales. We join the story as the hunt passes through Pembrokeshire hot on the heels of Twrch Trwyth and his piglets.

'So they set forth through the sea towards Wales. And Arthur and his hosts, his horses and his dogs, entered Prydwen (Arthur's ship), that they might encounter them without delay. Twrch Trwyth landed in Porth Cleis in Dyfed, and Arthur came to Mynyw. The next day it was told to Arthur that they had gone by, and he

94

overtook them as they were killing the cattle of Cynnwas Cwryfagyl, having slain all that were at Aber Gleddyf, of man and beast, before the coming of Arthur.

Now when Arthur approached, Twrch Trwyth went on as far as Preseleu, and Arthur and his hosts followed him thither, and Arthur sent men to hunt him; Eli and Trachmyr, leading Drutwyn the whelp of Greid the son or Eri, and Gwarthegyd the son of Caw, in another quarter, with the two dogs of Glythmyr Ledewig, and Bedwyr leading Cafall, Arthur's own dog. And all the warriors ranged themselves around the Nevern. And there came the three sons of Cleddyf Difwlch, men who had gained much fame at the slaying of Chief Boar Ysgithyrwyn; and they went on from Glyn Nyfer, and came to Cwm Cerwyn.

And there Twrch Trwyth made a stand, and slew four of Arthur's champions, Gwarthegyd the son of Caw, and Tarawc of Allt Clwyd, and Rheidwn the son of Beli Adfer, and Iscovan Hael. After he had slain these men, he made a second stand in the same place. And there he slew Gwydre the son of Arthur, and Garselit Wyddel, and Glew the son of Ysgawd, and Iscawyn the son of Panon; and there he himself was wounded.

And the next morning before it was day, some of the men came up with him. And he slew Huandaw, and Gogigwr, and Penpingon, three attendants upon Glewlwyd Gafaelfawr, so that Heaven knows, he had not an attendant remaining, excepting only Llaesgefyn, a man from whom no one ever derived any good. And together with these, he slew many of the men of that country, and Gwlydyn Saer, Arthur's chief Architect.

Then Arthur overtook him at Pelumyawc, and there he slew Madawc the son of Teithyon, and Gwyn the son of Tringad, the son of Neved, and Eiryawn Penllorau. Thence he went to Aberteifi, where he made another stand, and where he slew Cyflas the son of Cynan, and Gwilenhin King of France. Then he went as far as Glyn Ystu, and there the men and the dogs lost him.

Then Arthur summoned unto him Gwyn ap Nudd, and he asked him if he knew aught of Twrch Trwyth. And he said he did not.

And all the huntsmen went to hunt the swine as far as Dyffryn Llychwr. And Grugyn Silver Bristle, (his bristles were like silver wire, and whether he went through the wood or through the plain, he was to be traced by the glittering of his bristles,) and Llwydawg

95

Gofynnyad closed with them and killed all the huntsmen, so that there escaped but one man only. And Arthur and his hosts came to the place where Grugyn and Llwydawg were. And there he let loose the whole of the dogs upon them, and with the shout and barking that was set up, Twrch Trwyth came to their assistance.

And from the time that they came across the Irish sea, Arthur had never got sight of him until then. So he set men and dogs upon him, and thereupon Twrch started off and went to Mynydd Amanw. And there one of his young pigs was killed. Then they set upon him life for life, and Twrch Llawin was slain, and then there was slain another of the swine, Gwys was his name. After that Twrch went on to Dyffryn Amanw, and there Banw and Bennwig were killed. Of all his pigs there went with him alive from that place none save Grugyn Silver Bristle, and Llwydawg Gofynnyad.

Thence he went on to Llwch Ewin, and Arthur overtook him there, and he made a stand. And there Twrch slew Echel Forddwytwll, and Garwyli the son of Gwyddawg Gwyr, and many men and dogs likewise. And thence they went to Llwch Tawy. Grugyn Silver Bristle parted from them there, and went to Din Tywi. And thence he proceeded to Ceredigion, and Eli and Trachmyr with him, and a multitude likewise. Then he came to Garth Gregyn, and there Llwydawg Gofynnyad fought in the midst of them, and slew Rhudfyw Rhys and many others with him (and there Grugyn Silver Bristle was killed). Then Llwydawg went thence to Ystrad Yw, and there the men of Armorica met him, and there he slew Hirpeissawg the king of Armorica, and Llygatrudd Emys, and Gwrbothu, Arthur's uncles, his mother's brothers, and there was he himself slain.'

*The Mabinogion*, Lady Charlotte Guest

The Twrch Trwyth is then chased further along the coast of Wales until he is forced into the Severn estuary. There Arthur's men manage to dunk him into the sea and as they do the huntsman Mabon son of Modron seizes the razor and Cyledyr the Wild steals the shears. Twrch Trwyth manages to get upright though before they can get the comb from him and he runs into Cornwall causing more destruction and death until the comb is finally taken from him. Then, as a testimony to his powerful strength, he escapes Arthur and

96

his warriors and escapes into the sea with the last surviving two of his offspring.

As well as Twrch Trwyth there is another legend of a great boar who travelled throughout Wales. The story is found in the longest of the Welsh Triads, which tells of the 'Three Powerful Swineherds of the Isle of Britain'. Pryderi, who guards his Otherworld swine, is one of these swineherders, and the second is Tristan, another character from Welsh tradition. The third swineherder is named as Coll and he guards over an animal quite different from the docile Otherworld pigs of Pryderi, one that shows striking similarities with Twrch Trwyth.

The third (swineherder) was Coll son of Collfrewy with the swine of Dallwyr Dallben in Dallwyr's Glen in Cornwall. Now one of the swine was with young and Henwen was her name: and it was foretold that the Isle of Prydain would be the worse for her litter: and Arthur collected the host of Prydain and went about to destroy it. Then one sow went burrowing, and at the Headland of Hawstin in Cornwall she took to the sea with the swineherd following her. And in Maes Gwenith in Gwent she dropped a grain of wheat and a bee, and ever since Maes Gwenith is the best place for wheat and bees. And at Llonyon in Penfro she dropped a grain of barley and another of wheat: therefore the barley of Llonyon has passed into proverb. And on Rhiw Gyferthwch in Arfon she dropped a wolf-cub and an eagle chick. The wolf was given to Mergaed and the eagle to Breat, a prince from the North, and they were the worse for having them. And at Llanfair in Arfon, to wit below the Maen Du, she dropped a kitten, and from the Maen Du the swineherd cast it into the sea, but the sons of Paluc reared it to their detriment. It grew to be Cath Paluc, 'Palug's Cat,' and proved one of the three chief molestations of Mona reared in the island: the second was Daronwy and the third was Edwin king of England.'

John Rhys, *Celtic Folklore*

This story of Henwen belongs to the same tradition as the story of the hunt of Twrch Trwyth. The two tales seem to be related as both are hunted by Arthur and both run across Wales and Cornwall. The two tales mirror each other however as Henwen starts from

97

Cornwall and runs west across south Wales whereas Twrch Trwyth ran east through south Wales and into Cornwall.

Although Arthur hunts Henwen in this story it is interesting to see that in an earlier version of the same tale there is no mention of Arthur hunting the sow at all and Coll merely hangs onto her mane while she journeys through Wales. It is also possible that the hunting of Twrch was added later to the story of Culhwch as Ysbaddaden asks for another boar, Ysgithyrwyn to be hunted before Twrch and this story is quickly dealt with to make way for the overly long account of the hunt of the Twrch. It seems very likely therefore that the story of Twrch Trwyth once existed as an independent story. There were probably many similar tales of giant boars that were hunted by a variety of different Welsh heroes but they soon become overshadowed by the fame of Arthur and the Twrch Trwyth legend and became more and more similar to each other.

Henwen's name means 'Old White' and we have already seen that white animals were of Otherworld origin, like the dogs of Arawn. The fact that Henwen gives birth to wheat, bees, and barley indicates that she has taken a role of a culture goddess who brings forth riches from her womb. Not everything she creates is good though for she also brings forth the pests of the wolf cub and eagle-chick. The other pest that Henwen gives birth to, Palug's Cat, also appears in an early Welsh Arthurian poem where it goes on a rampage until Arthur's best warrior Cai finally manages to kill it.

One quite obvious aspect of this story of Henwen is the regional bias. She gives birth to wheat, bees and barley in south Wales, all of which are positive to have. To north Wales however she only gives birth to an eagle, a wolf and a kitten, which all turn out to be pests. The writer was therefore quite biased towards south Wales and he used the story to possibly play on a stereotype of the desolate mountainous north and the abundant plains of the south.

Like the tale of Henwen the story of the hunting of Twrch Trwyth is full of the names of places, heroes and Twrch's piglets. At first sight this may be pretty daunting to the reader but they are given because many of the events in the story are there to explain place-names. An example of this is the place where Twrch's piglet Grugyn Silver Bristle was killed in Ceredigion which is now known as Garth Gregyn, 'Grugyn's Hill'. These are called onomastic tales and in Irish legend there is a wide range of these stories called Dindshenchas and they gave short stories behind the naming of the hills, mountains, fords and other geographical features of Ireland.

Many of the place-names given enable us to trace Twrch Trwyth's travels through Pembrokeshire. He lands at Porth Cleis, now spelt Porthglais, a narrow inlet where the river Alun flows into the sea south of St Davids. Arthur stays at Mynyw, or St Davids, when he reaches Wales but the boar has already killed all the men and cattle in the area of Deu Gleddyf east of Haverfordwest. He then heads for Preseli, the mountain range in north Pembrokeshire, after which Arthur's warriors wait for him on the banks of the river Nyfer, or Nevern. Twrch then goes from Glyn Nyfer, the valley of the Nevern, to Cwm Cerwyn, a place-name which survives now in Foel Cwmcerwyn, the name of one of the mountains in the Preseli range. After a great slaughter there the boar runs to Penlumyawc, probably the area around Whitland between Llanddewi Velfrey and Laugharne. After this he heads across the estuary of the river Towy and into the neighbouring county of Carmarthenshire.

The story of Henwen also uses place-names in the narrative as the sow travels around Cornwall and Wales. The place in Pembrokeshire where she gives birth to the wheat and barley is given as Llonyon in Penfro and this is probably the same place as Lanion near Pembroke. The storyteller may have been trying to explain this place name with reference to the Welsh word 'Llawn' meaning 'full' (of wheat or abundance), but he is probably just giving a magical origin to the good agricultural land of Pembrokeshire.

The reason behind the existence of these stories about swine and boars is to be found in the high esteem given to the animal in Celtic tradition. We have already seen the story of how Pryderi's pigs originated from the Otherworld realm of Arawn and this link of swine and the gods is found frequently elsewhere. The Celts of Gaul had a swine god called Moccus and the boar features on coins, altars, figurines, bowls, helmets and trumpets. The meat of the pig was also a large contributory factor to its veneration and early Celtic burials commonly contain the remains of pig meat, given to the warriors for their Otherworld feast.

Traditions involving the meat of the animal are found in the Irish tales where the main part of the swine is called the 'Champion's

Portion' which the best hero claims at the feast. In the story of 'Bricriu's Feast' the three famed champions Cu Chulainn, Loegaire and Conall are all secretly told by the scheming Bricriu that the portion belongs to them as they are the best champion. All three warriors then claim the portion at the feast and this results in a long conflict of honour and superiority between the three. In another tale 'The Story of Mac Datho's Pig', the champions portion is a giant pig and by the end of the story one thousand and four hundred warriors die in the contest over the right to carve the pig. These tales show that the honour of eating the champion's portion was taken very seriously indeed.

These aspects of the boar cult are however not as important as the actual boar hunts in our two tales. Culhwch and Arthur hunted the Twrch Trwyth just like the Irish Finn and his warband hunted the terrible Balar's pig and the Fenians hunted the Torc Forbartach. In the story of Culhwch Ysbaddaden names another boar hunt as one of the tasks. Culhwch is to get the tusk of Chief Boar Ysgithyrwyn and this is soon accomplished by Caw of Scotland while he rides Arthur's horse. The story of the wild boar hunt was an important one. In the real world the hunt was a test of strength and manhood, but in legend it has ritual overtones for the boar is rarely killed and either leads the heroes to the Otherworld or through its power ravages whole countries.

The hunting of the Twrch Trwyth includes one other magical aspect. After Arthur himself unsuccessfully fights with Twrch his men go to Twrch Trwyth and ask him what he is. The boar answers that he was once a king who was transformed into a pig because of his wickedness. His name is given as 'Twrch son of the ruler Taredd' and Twrch himself says they have suffered enough by being turned into pigs without being hunted as well. This change from human to animal occurs elsewhere and an Irish hero called Diarmuid was forbidden to hunt boars because his half brother had been magically turned into a wild boar. The name of Henwen also occurs as a personal name, giving the suggestion that this sow may once have been a human transformed into an animal for some wrong doing. This punishment is best illustrated in the Mabinogi of Math where Gwydion and Gilfaethwy who were turned into a pig and a sow and made to mate with each other as punishment for the rape of Goewin.

100

In Irish tradition there is a boar called Torc Triath who is a direct parallel to the Welsh Twrch Trwyth. Torc Triath is called the king of the boars and he belongs to the Tuatha De Danaan, a family of Irish gods. This Irish boar king was a god and considering that Arthur and all his best warriors cannot kill Twrch Trwyth there is also a large element of godliness in the Welsh boar. The mythological roots of this tale seem to be of a boar god, or a human god transformed into a boar, who ravages the mortal world in anger. This was a useful tale-type that could attract various heroes who would prove their prowess by hunting it. The many different boar hunting stories show that this type of tale was very popular and the tales must have once had many more mythological associations that have not survived.

The medieval audiences of these boar hunt stories would have themselves heard about or taken part in real boar hunts and so the hugely exaggerated magical hunt tales would have been appreciated. Pembrokeshire, already associated with Pwyll's magical swine and their swineherder Pryderi, is again featured in the tales of Twrch and Henwen and there must have once been some special reason for the association of Pembrokeshire with magical swine. Both of the tales are also striking examples of how important geographical descriptions were in some traditional tales. It was important to the audience that these tales took place in familiar recognised places rather than the romantic 'never-never' land of modern folk stories. Both the tales of Henwen and Twrch Trwyth take us through a whirlwind tour of Pembrokeshire, back to a time when fierce animals roamed through people's villages as well as through their imaginations.

## Praising Tenby

From a poem in the ancient manuscript called the Book of Taliesin we get a unique glimpse of the type of place where many of the tales in this book would have been composed and told. The poem describes one of the fortresses of the Welsh kings of the dark ages and is called 'Etmic Dinbych', or 'Praising Tenby'. The Welsh name for Tenby is 'Dinbych y Pysgod', 'Little Fortress of the Fishes', and this is the Dinbych of the poem. All traces of this early fortress have unfortunately now been obliterated by the Norman castle which stands on Castle Hill in Tenby. This dark age fortress would have mainly consisted of earthen banks and defensive ditches with wooden buildings, storage pits and a hall inside. As all this physical evidence is now gone the poem gives us a rare glimpse into the world of tenth century Tenby.

The lord of Dinbych is named as Bleiddudd, which means 'Wolf Lord', a reference to the strength and ferocity of the animal. Bleiddudd is now dead however and the poet looks back to the past. He praises Bleiddudd's bravery and generosity and recalls the time when he slept near his lord in the court, enjoying the luxuries of life. The poet also recollects the sight of the warriors drinking and celebrating with their ale at feasts in the court. Bleiddudd's court is described as a coastal fort where white sea gulls flew overhead as waves crashed against the cliffs below:

> 'There is a fine fortress on a height,
> Lavish its feasting, loud its revelry.
> Beautiful all round it, that fort of champions,
> Is the flying spray: its wings are long!'

Ifor Williams, *The Beginnings of Welsh Poetry*

The bard who praises the fine stronghold and its noble lord also seems to have offended Bleiddudd in the past and he sings the poem as an appeal to his son, the new ruler, for clemency. This sort of poem of reconciliation appears quite frequently in Welsh poetry but unfortunately in this case we know nothing about the past events.

Amongst the descriptions and praise in the poem there is also a unique reference to a building in the fortress:

> 'The writings of Britain were the chief object of care,
> Where the waves make their roaring.
> Long may it remain, that cell I was wont to visit!'

Ifor Williams, *The Beginnings of Welsh Poetry*

This tells us that Bleiddudd's court was prosperous and cultured enough to have its own manuscripts stored in a cell, a sort of early library. The settlements of the Welsh lords at this time were not merely dirty, draughty 'barbarian' halls but cultured places where the court poet had to perform and compose almost daily. These manuscripts would have held the genealogies, histories and legends of the court. All of these, apart from this poem, are now lost. From these descriptions Tenby, or Dinbych, appears to be a well-established royal residence similar to Narberth in the Mabinogion.

Bleiddudd is not the only king that we know of from this era in Pembrokeshire. There are sparse clues, usually just names, that we have for other rulers. The placename Lochturffin in Mathry parish means 'The Pool of Triphun' and there are two early kings with this name, one who ruled in Dyfed around 520 AD and another who died in 814 AD. Cadifor Fawr, another early king of Dyfed, is remembered in the place-names Ffwrn Cadifor, 'Cadifor's Oven' and Cadifor Hall in Cilgerran and finally the earthwork of Old Castle near Manorbier has been identified with the Liscastell, 'Castle Court', of Aircol Lawhir a famous sixth century ruler of Dyfed.

The exact identification of Bleiddudd or his poet is obscure. There is a Bleiddudd named in the Welsh genealogies but it is uncertain whether it is the same figure. There is a place name of Treleddyd-fawr three kilometres north of St David's that contains the name Bleiddudd. It is on the other side of Pembrokeshire from Tenby but assuming that his lordship was of a reasonable size it could represent the site of his northern court. Apart from these sparse clues his son, his lordship and indeed his settlement at Tenby are all otherwise unknown. This poem therefore is very special in that it gives us a brief glimpse into this lost part of Pembrokeshire's history.

## King Arthur's Stones

Of all the Welsh kings of the past the most well known throughout the world is Arthur. Like the ferocious boar Twrch Trwyth, Arthur became associated with the Welsh landscape through numerous legends. His fame spread far and wide throughout Wales and even today he has places named after him in Pembrokeshire. In medieval times and earlier it became customary to call large or exceptional features after well known figures like Arthur, St Samson or the Devil himself and in this way Arthur became regarded in popular imagination as a giant of a man in the literal sense.

The shape of the capstones on some megalithic burial chambers gave rise to the popular notion that these disk shaped stones, sometimes weighing many tons, were thrown there like a quoit by Arthur. The game of quoits became popular in the 16th century and so many burial chambers, like the well known Pentre Ifan in Cemais, became known as Coetan Arthur, 'Arthur's Quoit'. Most of these megaliths have no surviving story attached to them and only the large capstone remains still lying where Arthur threw it. Examples of this are the Coetan Arthur east of Newtown, the Coetan Arthur near Manorbier and the now lost Coetan Arthur in Llanllawer parish.

Some of these megaliths do still have small legends attached to them and one of these Coetan Arthurs is also known as Carn Arthur or 'Arthur's Cairn'. It is one of a series of Arthurian place names in the Preseli Mountains near Mynachlog-Ddu. The stones of this monument are also very special because they are bluestones from the nearby ancient quarry that produced the stones for the inner circle at Stonehenge. This Coetan was said to have been thrown there by Arthur from the stone circle of Dyffryn Stones which is over eight kilometres away to the south west. Other Arthurian names have sprung up elsewhere as there is an Eisteddfa Arthur, 'Arthur's Seat', just north of the Preseli mountains near Brynberian and on a farm called Pen Arthur, itself on St Davids Head, is a burial chamber called Coetan Arthur.

Arthur, like other famous heroes, was in popular imagination often associated with other megalithic and bronze age monuments. This belief began very early on and a good example is Stonehenge which in medieval times was said to have been constructed by Merlin. In Preseli on the same mountain as Carn Arthur is Bedd Arthur, 'Arthur's Grave', and the whole mountain is so full of cairns that the local people called it Mynydd Carn, 'Cairn Mountain'. These monuments are said to have been built in memory of the heroes of age old battles and Arthur is counted as one of these warriors. Below one of the ends of Mynydd Carn are two standing stones that are called Cerrig Meibion Arthur, 'The Stones of Arthur's Sons'. These stones are said to remember the sons of Arthur who were killed in a now unknown battle in the area.

The mountainous landscape of the north, and especially the area of the Preseli hills is full of cairns and other prehistoric monuments. It also has a complex of Arthurian place names but as no substantial pieces of legend survive it is hard to see the origins of these. The legends could be ancient or they could merely be popular medieval associations. We must remember that the prehistoric monuments named after Arthur would have commemorated dead warriors of the area who lived centuries before Arthur. This ancient landscape, full of mysterious memorials to long gone warriors, must have long been a breeding ground for legends about the ancient Arthur.

## Gwalchmai and Walwyn's Cast

As well as the great king himself the heroes of Arthurian legend became associated with Pembrokeshire. Arthur's group of heroic champions, who later became the knights of English and French literature, feature in Welsh legends more than the great king himself. In Welsh tradition one of Arthur's best known champions was Gwalchmai who, in the Arthurian romance tales, later became the English Sir Gawain and the French Gauvains. His origins however belong in Welsh tradition where he was called:

'Gwalchmai the son of Gwyar...he never returned home without achieving the adventure of which he went in quest. He was the best of footmen and the best of knights. He was nephew to Arthur, the son of his sister, and his cousin.'

*The Mabinogion*, Lady Charlotte Guest

Gwalchmai's name probably means 'The Hawk of the Plain' and as Arthur's cousin he was the example of bravery and honour. He was not all brawn and no brains though for he was also a wise champion and in the Welsh romances he features as Arthur's peacemaker and this earned him the title of one of the 'Three Golden-Tongued Knights' of Arthur's court due to his eloquence.

The county of Pembrokeshire is involved in the story of Gwalchmai through the writings of William of Malmesbury. William in 1125 AD called Gwalchmai 'Walwen' and he stated that during the reign of William the Conqueror the grave of Arthur's cousin Walwen was to be found in the province of Rhos, one of the seven ancient cantrefs that made up Dyfed. It was found upon the sea shore and the grave itself was said to have been fourteen feet long.

This grave is also mentioned in Welsh sources in the ancient Englynion y Beddau, or Grave Poems. The poem says that his grave is in Peryddon 'as a reproach to men' and this may refer to a tradition that Gwalchmai was treacherously killed by his fellow men. William of Malmesbury says that he knew of two accounts of how Walwen met his death. One said that he was killed after being wounded and shipwrecked by his enemies and the other said he was killed by his fellow men at a banquet. Treacherous and tragic deaths often occurred in Celtic literature and this is probably one of the many lost legends of Wales.

The two traditions, the Welsh poem and William's account, differ however on the point of where the grave was to be found. The Welsh source names Peryddon while William names the province of Rhos. The Peryddon named in the Welsh poem appears as a name for the river Dee in north Wales but there is now no Peryddon in the Rhos area of Pembrokeshire. There is however a connection between the two sources for a tenth century poem names an Aber Peryddon in South Wales. If this Peryddon was the old name for Sandyhaven Pill which starts at Castell Gwalchmai then the two sources would match. The grave of Gwalchmai could have been on the floodplain of the river Peryddon and therefore on the coast of the cantref of Rhos.

Even if this is wrong there is another good reason to place Gwalchmai in Pembrokeshire as there is a Castell Gwalchmai, Gwalchmai's Castle, in the same area, a substantial hillfort that may be Iron Age in origin. In Ireland many hillforts are named after the ancient legendary heroes who were supposed to have lived and ruled in them and a site close to Castell Gwalchmai offers a closer parallel. Cilgerran castle at Cardigan on the river Teifi has associations with Geraint, another of Arthur's knights. The site was named Dyn Gereint or 'Geraint's Castle' up until the eleventh century and this Geraint features in the Welsh romance of 'Geraint and Enid' which tells of his adventures.

So we have two pieces of evidence about Gwalchmai's association with the Roose hundred in south-west Pembrokeshire.

106

One tradition tells of his death on the seashore and another place name hints at his life at Castell Gwalchmai. There would have probably once been a series of stories about Gwalchmai told in Pembrokeshire but now all that remains are the brief allusions of William's account and the solitary grave poem. Other hillfort names like Castell Cadw, 'The Castle of Cadw', also suggest lost associations with Welsh characters but, apart from poems like the one on Tenby already described further information about these hillforts rarely survive.

## Giants

Arthur was not the only giant who threw huge boulders from place to place. St Samson was said to have thrown Carreg Samson in Llanfrynach from the top of Frenni Fawr in Preseli. Another capstone in Dewsland is called Ffust Samson, or 'Samson's Flail' and Samson's Marble is a boulder on Cefn Garth in Cilgerran that he seems to have been fond of playing with. Apart from these men, whose fame outgrew their real stature, there was once a wholly different class of stone throwers in Pembrokeshire, the real giants.

In the Mabinogion tales are told of terrible giants like Ysbaddaden the Chief Giant and these creatures were an important feature of Celtic myth. Unfortunately in Pembrokeshire these giant tales have only survived as short folk tales which associated the giant with a particular place, usually a mountain. Mynydd Carningli is such a mountain. It is covered with many ancient remains such as cairns, hut circles and standing stones. The cairn is said to have been named after the giant Ingli who was probably also considered as the creator of many of the mountain's ancient monuments.

There are remnants of a tale about a giant known as Llyffant in north Pembrokeshire. He appears in a triad as one of the giants whose wives were killed 'with stealth' by Arthur. His home is to be found in the parish of Orllwyn Teifi at Castell Nant-y-garan which is a Norman motte. There is also a Castell-y-garn and a burial chamber near the farm of Trellyffaint which could be related to this giant legend. The burial chamber was probably thought of as his work. Trellyffaint is also associated with the toad legend by Gerald of Wales given later on in this chapter, giving the possibility that

107

two tales have been mixed up.

The antiquarian Richard Fenton during his tour of Pembrokeshire came across a legend of a giant's grave being found south-west of Cardigan near Trefigan in Nevern. He describes that many graves made of purple slabs were found. One of these contained a skeleton much larger than an ordinary man's with a giant sword by its side. Fenton wrote that the sword was so big that the tallest man in the area would not have been able to sheathe it. The dimensions of the coffin were probably exaggerated and although many giant skeletons are said to have been found in bronze age tumuli this site was probably an old Christian or iron age burial site.

Although giants were often associated with the megaliths and boulders they threw from hills unfortunately not many of their names have survived. There was a megalith at a farm called Goitan in Llanwnda parish which was said to have been thrown by a giant from a hill a kilometre to the north near Bristgarn. This sort of tale, like those of King Arthur and St Samson were frequently used to explain how the large standing stones and megaliths came to be in such strange places. It is a good example of how folklore and legend explain strange oddities like the megaliths by creating even stranger things like giants to account for them.

## Beddau

The Welsh word beddau means 'graves' and the final resting place of a hero was a very important place in Celtic society. What are now the archaeological remains of cairns and burial chambers in Pembrokeshire would once been the subject of a whole body of traditional lore concerning the exploits of the dead buried within them. In Welsh tradition there is a series of short poems called the beddau stanzas which tell of the grave sites of the ancient Welsh heroes. Most of these grave sites are now unknown but as we have seen with Pryderi's grave a few of the traditional graves can still be located. These give us a glimpse of a time when almost every pile of stones, like Bedd Arthur and the other cairns atop the Preseli Mountains, would have been a living monument to some hero's bravery.

Most of these heroes are forgotten now and so often completely different legends have sprung up around these traditional grave sites. Near the village of Brynberian in the north of Pembrokeshire is a place-name that provides a local example of the widespread tale of the Afanc. The Afanc was a fierce water monster who lived in lakes and pools and was prone to bursting the waters of its lakes and drowning whole towns. The local people were not very happy about having an Afanc living nearby and so they usually tried to rid themselves of it. The monster was so large and fearful that it had to be dragged away by chains and oxen after its watery home was drained. It seems the people of Brynberian once managed to catch one of these Afancs in a pool near the bridge. They buried the monster in a tumulus on a nearby hill and this is why the chambered cairn near the Nevern stream is now known as Bedd yr Afanc, 'The Afanc's Grave.'

There is a strange grave near Llanwnda that is in a natural hollow between two rocky outcrops. Here is a cromlech known as Carreg Samson named after the eminent St Samson who threw it from the top of Carn Fawr hillfort. He threw this great rock using only one finger and so the site was called Bedd Bys Mawr Samson, 'The Grave of Samson's Thumb'. There is also a standing stone called Bedd Morris in Cemais which was so named because it was where a robber known as Maurice was killed and buried. There are many other sites that are now without legends like Carn Gwr, 'The Hero's Carn', and Cerrig Marchogion, 'The Knight's Mound', in Cemais. Both of these are now shadows of the time when the grave sites of the ancient heroes would have been widely known.

## Magical Stones

Although unmoving and silent the rocks and stones of the earth, have a great ability to attract tales and legends. Burial chambers, standing stones and inscribed stones, together with weird and wonderful stones have all become the subject of people's imagination. Most of these stones were immovable, almost eternal, and so over generations they became well known features in the landscape, as familiar as the mountains and rivers. These stone monuments were however still markedly different from the natural features of the land because they had been shaped and placed by long-forgotten hands. These lost monument makers have, after thousands of years in their graves, since become the giants and magic men of legend.

The oldest of these stones, in terms of man's influence, must be the burial chambers or cromlechs. Sites like Pentre Ifan and Garn Gilfach near Llanwnda were built as tombs for the dead in the Stone Age. Their construction involved a large amount of effort by the people and even today they serve to remind us what can be achieved with just our hands, muscles and will. These places retained some of their sanctity in later ages through their associations with the legendary figures of Arthur, St Samson and the giants who became the supernatural forces behind these constructions.

Other stones were named after famous figures. The placename St Peter's Finger in Arberth may refer to a lost standing stone and in the Anglicised south of Pembrokeshire there are many 'Harold's Stones' to be found. Holy men have a special connection with stones through placenames like Carreg Samson and Carn Padrig. There are also others like Carn Wnda named after St Gwyndaf and Carreg Gybi named after St Cybi. It is possible that the saints used these stones for meeting places to hold sermons. Originally many sites, like the destroyed stone tombs of Maenclochog, Nine Wells and Fynnondridian, were once closely associated with holy wells and whatever pagan rituals occurred at these sites were soon Christianised and brought under the influence of the saints.

One side effect of this Christianisation of standing stones and burial chambers was that many became renamed and rededicated to a very well known figure, the devil himself. A burial chamber in Castlemartin and a standing stone in Stackpole are both called 'The Devils Quoit' and he seems to have taken over from older traditions about giants and heroes. The stones associated with Arthur, St Samson or the Devil are mainly ancient standing stones and cromlechs and it would be very interesting to know whether these stones were previously dedicated to the heroes and gods of pagan times.

The standing stones near Stackpole as well as being called Devils Quoits were once known as the Dancing Stones of Stackpole. As with many standing stones there was a tradition that on one special day they would come alive and go to the nearby Sais Ford to dance, later returning to their original positions as if nothing had happened. There is another tradition of moving stones in the parish of Llangan. While the local church was being built the builders left the stones

111

here at a field called Parc y Fonwent, 'The Churchyard Field'. Something decided however that this was not the proper place for the church and during the night a mysterious force moved the stones to the site of the present church. While this happened voices were heard in the dark saying 'Llangan, dyma'r fan' which means 'Llangan, here is the place'.

Rocks like Carreg yr Esgob, 'The Bishop's Stone', and Carn Cynon, 'Cynon's Rock' possibly once had tales that associated them with their namesakes but which are now lost. A more recent example of this is Carnedd Meibion Owen, 'The Rocks of the Sons of Owen' in Cemais. This placename is linked with an Elizabethan tale showing that stones have been the ongoing subject of stories and legends for many centuries. Through the ages stones were not just named after characters; many are simply called after the birds that rest on them like Carreg yr Eos, 'The Nightingale's Rock', and Carn y Fran, 'The Crow's Rock'. Other stones are named after their physical properties like Carreg Wastad, 'Smooth Stone' and Maen Sigl, 'Shaking Stone'.

Some stones had special qualities and through their names, like the cromlech known as Maen Dedwydd, 'The Blessed Stone', we can see that they must have once bestowed special powers. Another stone of this type has given its name to the town and parish of Maenclochog. The tale says that there was a stone close to the church, which was possibly the remains of a cromlech, and this stone rang like a bell when struck. The ringing would not stop until water from the nearby well of Ffynnon Fair was taken into the parish church. This special ability led the curious locals to break up the stone but they found nothing and now the only stones to be found at Maenclochog are the two inscribed stones in the church which commemorate two brothers from the 5th or 6th century called Andagellus and Coimagnus.

Mesur y Dorth is a name given to two special inscribed stones in Pembrokeshire. One is still set into a wall at Croesgoch on the road from St Davids to Fishguard and another was once set into the wall at the farm of Penarthur. The latter stone once stood with two other inscribed stones around the holy well at Penarthur and is now in St Davids Cathedral. The stones have inscribed ring-crosses on them and they became known as Mesur y Dorth, 'The Measure of the Loaf', due to the tradition that these quartered circles were once

112

used as a measurement for loaves of bread. Dewi is said to have been responsible for making the crosses so that he could regulate the supply of bread in times of famine.

The Mesur y Dorth stones are only two of the many inscribed stones in the county. Due to its early Irish settlement and position on the trade routes Pembrokeshire has the highest concentration of Ogham and early Christian stones in Wales. Many of these were associated with churches or were moved to churchyards later on for safekeeping and so it is not too difficult to visit a good selection. Ogham and Latin stones can be seen at most churches especially those at Clydai, Maenclochog, Llanllawer and Brawdy. St Davids cathedral also houses a fine selection but the most exquisitely elaborate stones, covered from top to bottom with elaborate knotwork, are those at Nevern church, Carew castle and Penally church near Tenby.

Gerald of Wales describes a plain but nevertheless significant stone in his book on the Conquest of Ireland that was completed in 1189 A.D. It was known as the Llech Lafar, 'The Speaking Stone' and it bridged the River Alun on the north side of St Davids cathedral. Gerald described the stone as being marble, 10 feet long, 6 feet wide, 1 foot deep and polished smooth by the feet of the faithful. Gerald says that there was a legend about this stone that was ancient when he wrote 800 years ago in the 12th century. One day when a corpse was being carried across the stone to the graveyard the stone burst into speech and then cracked down the middle. Gerald does not say what the stone said but the crack was still there in his day and no corpse was ever taken over it after that.

The main story about the Llech Lafar occurred when King Henry II of England encountered it as he was returning from his invasion of Ireland. The king disembarked from his ship at St Davids and went to the cathedral to pray with the church canons. As they walked a local woman threw herself at the king's feet and voiced a complaint about the bishop of St Davids. An interpreter told the king what the woman had said but the grievance could not, or would not, be dealt with. The woman got angry at this and shouted loudly for the Llech Lafar to revenge the crowd and all of the Welsh people against the king.

The crowd dragged her away from the king but as they did so she shouted louder, furiously reminding everyone of the prophecy that

Merlin had once made. He had said that an English king who had conquered Ireland would be wounded by a man with a red hand and would die on his way home as he passed St Davids and crossed the Llech Lafar. The king must have known of this prophecy for when he reached the stone he stopped before crossing. Then he walked straight across it and, reaching the other side, he turned to gaze at the stone saying 'Merlin is a liar, who will trust him now?' With this some say a member of the crowd pretended to be insulted and replied 'Well, you are obviously not the one who will conquer Ireland! Merlin was not talking about you!'

As the tradition of the Llech Lafar was very old even in Geralds time the stone was possibly one of the original features of the site of St Davids from when it was first established. An inscribed stone called the Sagranus Stone from St Dogmaels was also re-used as a bridge. It reputedly haunted by a white lady and it was also unlucky to touch the stone after dark. The Llech Lafar may have once been a standing stone or part of a megalithic tomb before being used as a bridge as stones of this kind were often re-used. All these varied traditions about stones shows their importance at the time. Standing stones, burial chambers and inscribed stones were regarded by the local community as magical, mystical and ancient objects and these attitudes are reflected in the stories about them. From the talking Llech Lafar stone to the highly crafted Carew Cross these stones are objects that lived and breathed through the legends told of them.

## Hen Ci Bal

At Dinas Head on the coast of North Pembrokeshire there are some steps in the rock of the cliffs known as Ol Traed y Bal 'The Bal's Footprints' because they resemble the tracks of a giant. Bal was once a famous giant in the area but the tradition of his vicious dog seems to have outlived him. The hideous creature was known in Pembrokeshire as Hen Ci Bal, 'Bal's Old Dog' and this monstrous dog was pitch black in colour with a thick chain around his neck that crashed and rattled with each movement of his massive body. If people were unfortunate to come across the huge beast its huge eyes would catch them in their frightful stare.

There is a story of a sailor who was on his way home one night after drinking in Fishguard when Hen Ci Bal came roaring for him,

114

ready to take his soul away. He was only saved from death by begging God for mercy and, after escaping, he vowed to lead a wholesome life (which he managed for short while at least). The Hen Ci Bal is also said to wait for sinners to die, wandering up and down their village until it is time to take their souls below the earth. Belief in this was once so strong that people were warned not to go outside while a sick person lay seriously ill in case the dog was waiting for the soul of the sinner. When people died there was also a belief that their souls entered the nearest water on their journey to heaven. The Hen Ci Bal therefore especially waited along the banks of the nearest river, for when the poor person died the dog would catch their souls before they could enter the water and escape. Legends of 'Devil Dogs' are found throughout Wales and they came to the sinful to drag their souls kicking and screaming to hell. A man from Pembrokeshire, out for a walk one day was once thrown over a hedge by one of these dogs and so the next time he ventured to the spot he took a fighting dog with him. This dog was soon crouching in terror however for on the path in front of them appeared the apparition of a huge snarling devil dog. The origins of these fearsome dogs may lie in tales of dogs from the Otherworld, such as those belonging to Arawn in the tale of Pwyll but the Hen Ci Bal seems to have also originated as the terrible pet of an equally fearful giant.

### The Killer Toads of Cemais

Gerald of Wales in his book 'The Journey Through Wales' which was written in the late 12th century relates a strange tale from Cemais that he heard as he travelled through north Pembrokeshire. Here there was once a man who had been taken ill and was then mysteriously persecuted by toads. The creatures swarmed all around him as he lay in his sick bed and even though his friend killed whole hosts of them they could not be stopped. They came in large numbers from all directions aiming straight for him and soon enough the people who defended him were worn out from killing them.

The man's friends had an idea of how to get him away from the toads and to this end they stripped a tree of its leaves and branches and hoisted him to the top of the trunk wrapped in a bag. The toads however merely climbed up the trunk and promptly ate him all, leaving only his bones in the bag. The man was called Seisyll Esgairhir or 'Seisyll Longshanks' and Gerald explains the story as being a strange example of God's justice against the wicked.

This tale, when Gerald came across it, may have been a short anecdote to explain the place name of Trellyffaint, a few kilometres north of Nevern, which means 'Toad Farm'. The origins of the story however may be related to the name George Owen gives for Dinas Island in his 'Description of Pembrokeshire'. He calls the island Ynys Bach Llyffan Gawr, 'The Island of the Giant Toad' and this could refer to a legend of a giant toad that was later confused to create the tale of Seisyllt. The tale is also possibly related to the tradition of the giant Llyffant, mentioned already in the giants section. The identity of the poor man who was eaten by the toads is a mystery but there is a Tre-Seisyllt, 'Seisyllt's Town', not too far away in Dewsland and a Tre Seissyllt-fach near Fishguard, and both of these place names could be related to this strange tale.

The toads of Cemais tale illustrates well the great variety of tradition that must have once existed in Pembrokeshire. At the same time the confusing state of some of them reminds us that their origins and the meanings are often forgotten or buried so deep that we can never hope to fully understand them. The tales, as we have them now, are a magical mix of legend, mythology, religion, and imagination that came together to create stories that would puzzle and amaze people. The only subject that now remains unexplored is the intriguing world of the Tylwyth Teg, the Welsh fairies.

116

# Chapter four

## The Tylwyth Teg

The Tylwyth Teg are a magical race that are as old as the hills and mountains of Wales. Throughout the ages they have crossed over into our world to influence the affairs of mankind, sometimes for the better, sometimes for the worst. Their existence is widespread throughout the Celtic countries and they appear as the Cornish Piskies, the Irish Sidhe, and the Phynodderree from the Isle of Man. The English call them the fairies and they are known in Nordic tradition as goblins and elves. In Wales they are the Tylwyth Teg, 'The Fair Family', or Bendith y Mamau, 'The Mother's Blessing' and they were once very close to the hearts and minds of many of the Cymry.

The original Otherworld inhabitants were characters like Arawn, Bran and Rhiannon but through time the Otherworld people became the Tylwyth Teg, the diminutive figures of folk tradition. It is this mixture of ancient legend and folk belief that gave birth to the 'fairy' stories of the Tylwyth Teg. These tales evolved organically throughout time, picking up new influences and dropping sections that had lost their relevance. The main characteristics of the Tylwyth Teg however were so important that they were never forgotten and their traits are quite cohesive throughout all of the Celtic countries. These tales of the Pembrokeshire tribe of the Tylwyth Teg are curious concoctions where the weird and the sublime occur within the everyday world.

## Rhys the Deep

In the area around Cardigan the fairies were known as Plant Rhys Ddwfn, 'The Children of Rhys the Deep'. This name grew from the belief that there was a lost cantref in the sea between Cemais in Pembrokeshire and the Lleyn peninsula in north Wales. Rhys Ddwfn, a similar figure to the Otherworld lord Arawn, was the ruler of this land and the inhabitants were known as his 'children'. His mythical cantref was described by the sailors of Pembrokeshire as the green meadows of the fairy islands. These islands were only briefly visible to mortals before they vanished but there are legends

117

from the beginning of the 19th century of men who landed on these ever changing islands, only to find out that they were fairy islands when they returned to their boats and saw them disappear.

Rhys Ddwfn's children are described as handsome people who were small in stature. They managed to keep their lands invisible to strangers because of the magical properties of the strange herbs that grew on their islands. Their home could only be seen from the places where these magic herbs grew and there was only one such spot in Cemais, one square yard of turf, where they grew outside of the fairy islands. To find this magic spot you had to search alone and if you found it you had to stand perfectly still, for if you moved the vision vanished and you would be unable to find it again. Some people also say that at Llanon on the north coast of Dewsland there was another spot from where the islands could be seen.

A later Christianised tradition of how mortals could get to see these islands concerns the churchyard of St Davids. If you took a turf from the churchyard and stood on it on the shore you would soon see the marvellous islands out to sea. One man who did this immediately put to sea to find the islands, only to lose sight of them when left the land. He returned to the turf, saw where they were again, and set out in his boat once more only to find that the islands disappeared again. The third time he had a clever idea. He took the turf from the land and stood on it in his boat so he could clearly see the islands until he stepped onto them from his boat, never to be seen again.

The continuing belief in these fairy islands off Pembrokeshire led to some sightings that seem to have nothing to do with fairy stories. One ship's captain on a summer morning was passing Grassholm island in deep water when on one side of the ship he saw thick meadow. This land covered a large piece of the sea and was lying just below the water with its grass waving in the tides. The scientific attitudes of the last century also sought for explanations of the belief in fairy lands. A friend of the folklorist who recorded the tale of Llech y Derwydd in this chapter took him to the top of Garn Fawr in Llanwnda parish. Here the sun's rays made the mirage of a golden countryside out in the sea and he considered this to be the reason why people believed in the fairy islands.

The Otherworld islands are one of the fundamental beliefs of Celtic mythology. They are at the same time real and mythical

118

places and we have seen in the Mabinogion how one of these places was named as Gwales. This island was the setting for 'The Entertainment of the Noble Head', when the magical decapitated head of the god Bran entertained his friends after a disastrous battle. Here they had all sorts of food laid before them and they did not grow weary. This Gwales is said to be the tiny island of Grassholm that lies seven miles west of Skomer off the south-west coast of Pembrokeshire. This tradition is very significant because islands off the south-west coast of Ireland and the west coast of Scotland were also thought of in Celtic tradition as Otherworld islands.

The Welsh god Bran had an Irish counterpart, also called Bran, who once had a vision of a beautiful Otherworld woman who lived on an island. He took to the sea in a coracle to visit the islands and meet her. Bran and his companions soon found the 'Island of Woman' where the food was never ending and gave the eater whatever taste they desired. This story, 'The Voyage of Bran', is over a thousand years old and the worship of this Celtic god probably goes back well into the centuries before the birth of Christ. The ancient accounts of the Irish Bran's voyage and the entertaining of the Welsh Bran's head on Gwales show that the traditions of mysterious fairy islands off the Pembrokeshire coast and the real islands themselves both have an ancient mythological significance.

The belief in these coastal islands also led people to believe that the Tylwyth Teg used underground caves and tunnels to travel from their land to the coast of West Wales. This was said to be how the fairies frequented the markets on the coast and in 1896 a woman from Fishguard swore in the fairies existence and said she knew that they went to Haverfordwest market to buy their goods. Certain markets were patronised frequently by the fairies who spent their silver pennies and there was one butcher at Milford Haven whom they bought from again and again, presumably because he was a fair man. Once some farmers in Cardigan wanted to profit from the fairies, who visited the market often, and so they increased their corn prices. The fairies were not pleased with this at all and were never seen there again, preferring to go to Fishguard market from then on.

# The Otherworld

The Otherworld was also an abstract place and the tradition stayed alive in the hearts and stories of the people of Wales more than any other theme. The belief in the fairy Otherworld had itself come from the Otherworld of the gods, called Tir Na Nog in Ireland and known as Annwn in the tale of Pwyll. Tales of how mortal men and women went to this mystical Otherworld to enjoy its fruits were very popular. This crossing over of the fairyworld into the mortal world occurs frequently both in recent folk tales and in the great ancient Celtic legends. The outcomes of these tales were never assured though and while some ended in happiness and good fortune others ended in immense pain and suffering.

Some of the visits to the fairy world were wondrous, life changing events and a folklorist recorded this tale from an old woman who lived near the Pentre Ifan burial chamber in the parish of Nevern. She had heard a lot about the fairies in her lifetime and she had also heard of many people who had seen the fairies dancing around the burial chamber. The folklorist describes how he sat down with the woman and her niece and nephew in the warmth of the fire and listened to her stories for two nights in a row. This experience could not take place now and we must thank W. Evans-Wentz for recording this tale of how a shepherd boy's visit to the Otherworld folk led to them being known as the Tylwyth Teg.

One cloudy and misty day a poor shepherd boy called Einion lost his way in the mountains and wandered around for hours without knowing where he was. After a long while he came to a hollow in the ground surrounded by rushes and here he saw a number of round rings in the grass. He knew the danger of the fairy rings as he had heard of other shepherds who had walked into them and never returned he so tried to get as far away from the place as possible. His efforts were hopeless however for he could not find his way out of the place and found himself wandering around blindly in the fog.

Suddenly a man appeared from out of the fog. The shepherd was not too frightened at this because the old man had gleaming blue eyes and looked like a merry old soul. He kept on walking past the young boy and Einion resolved to follow him. As he did so the man turned to him and, with his blue eyes glaring, said to the boy 'Do not say a word until I tell you!' The boy nodded and soon became quite frightened as he walked behind the old man along the mountain. When they reached a standing stone the old man walked up to it and, after tapping it three times, lifted it up effortlessly to reveal a path leading deep into the ground.

The path shone with a white light and a flight of steps appeared which descended down deep into the earth. The man turned to Einion again with his blue eyes shining and said 'Follow me!' before disappearing down the dark hole. Einion followed and it seemed as if they only walked for a short while. When they emerged from the tunnel, there stretched out before Einion was a beautiful wooded land where clear blue rivers ran like snakes through green meadows. Amidst all this beauty the man led him to a handsome palace where delightful birdsong enchanted him and bade him enter.

The palace was made of gold and shining white marble and music floated around every room. The boy started to notice that there were no people around but soon enough a meal of tender meat and sweet wine appeared from nowhere and, after he had finished the meal, it disappeared again. Within a few days Einion heard voices around the palace but he saw no-one apart from the old man who came one day to tell him that he was now allowed to speak. Einion tried to ask the man questions but when he opened his mouth not a sound would come out as his tongue was stuck fast and would not move.

Just as he was wondering what trouble he had gotten himself into an old lady full of smiles entered the room with three beautiful young women trailing behind her. The young women also smiled and as soon as they saw Einion they all rushed over to him and started to ask him all sorts of questions. They soon saw that he could not reply so one of the women leant over and kissed him gently on his lips and this loosened his tongue. He talked with the beautiful women at length and while he was in the magical palace he enjoyed every luxury that he could possibly think of.

A year and a day went by but it felt like he had only been there for a day as there was no sense of time in the palace. Although he was happy and content he soon felt a longing for his home, family and friends and so he politely asked the old man if he could leave the palace and go back to his world again. The old man asked him to wait a little while and soon he found out the cause for his request. The girl who liked Einion the best out of the three sisters came to

121

him the next day saying that she was worried that if he left he would never return. The shepherd boy promised the fairy woman that he would return and (because in the Otherworld a promise is as good as done) she let him go and even gave him gifts for his time away.

The boy was quite unaware that back home he had been sorely missed by his family. His strange disappearance had led to another shepherd being accused of his murder and this shepherd had fled away to America to escape being punished. When Einion arrived back not one of his family or friends knew him at first for he had been gone so long but soon he managed to fit back into his old life and enjoyed seeing all the people and places that he had missed once more.

It was at the next new moon that the boy suddenly became reminded of his promise to the fairy woman. He left as soon as possible and was well received on his return to the palace. Olwen, his fairy woman, was there to great him. She was smiling broadly, glad that he had come back. Einion felt so much love for her that they vowed to get married and so, as the fairies are not ones for pompous ceremony or unnecessary noise, they got married secretly and almost in silence. When they were united Einion asked her to join him in the real world where they could make a new life for themselves. Olwen gladly accepted and her family blessed them with a gift of two pure white ponies.

They went with the gifts to Einion's world and because they had easy access to the abundant riches of the Otherworld they soon acquired a large estate. They lived very happily together and a son was born to them whom they named Taliesin. Soon people came to ask about Olwen's background and pedigree but as she could not give them one she avoided the questions. People thought that she was from the fairy lands because of this and they asked the shepherd if it was true. Einion told them this, 'there is no doubt she is one of them for she has two sisters as beautiful as herself. When you see them all together you would surely call them fair-folk' and because of these words the people from then on always knew the fairies as the Tylwyth Teg or the 'Fair Folk'.

This story contains the ancient motif of the mortal who marries someone from the Otherworld. It is a very common tale in Welsh folklore and it reflects the time when the heroes of legends often married into the families of the Celtic gods to produce gifted and powerful offspring. Although no details are given of the child of Einion and the fairy this folk tale is a more recent version of the ancient legends. Pwyll married the Otherworld goddess Rhiannon to produce the hero Pryderi and the most famous Irish hero Cu Chulainn was also born from the union of Dechtire the mortal and the sun god Lug.

The Otherworld, whether in folklore or legend, was always the divine source of all things new and magical, like the magic swine that Pwyll received from Arawn, and the children produced from the Otherworld were especially gifted with magical strength or knowledge. Not far away in Carmarthenshire there is a legend of a lake fairy who marries a mortal man and although they break up and she goes back to the Otherworld her children stay in this world. They are taught by their mother in the arts of the Otherworld and gifted with this magic her sons became the famed Physicians of Myddfai, a family who were known all over Wales for centuries as great doctors. The Taliesin in the story, as the son of Einion and Olwen, must have been also fated for greatness but unfortunately we hear no more of him.

## The Fountain of Knowledge and Temptation

The Otherworld and the fairy islands were the lands of the ever-living where people lived a luxurious life free from worry, hunger or death. The people of Wales kept up this pagan belief long after they were Christianised and well into the last century. The fairy Otherworld of folklore was a place of luxury where everyone and everything was beautiful and the wine and fine food flowed freely. Although people like Einion found their happiness in the Otherworld it was not always a good place for mortals as the next two stories will show. The Otherworld was an immortal world and the people who went there always took their mortality along with them and this mixture was a very potent and unstable one.

The first story concerns another shepherd boy of only twelve years of age. He was tending his father's flocks on Frenifach mountain near the village of Crymych one fine morning in June and had driven the sheep for pasture. As he paused in his work he looked to the mountain of Frenifawr to see what the weather would bring for it was well known that the fog of this mountain had a peculiar property. If it fell to the Pembrokeshire side it forecast fair weather and likewise if it fell to the Cardiganshire side it would bring foul weather. He didn't even get to notice the fog though for he saw a party of soldiers going about some urgent business nearby.

Thinking it was strange to see soldiers marching so early in the morning he gazed closer at the figures. They looked too small to be normal men and, with his curiosity building, he climbed to a place where he could have a better view. He soon saw that they were the Tylwyth Teg and he knew straight away that his parents would never believe what he was seeing. He thought about running back to tell them but he knew that by the time he returned the Tylwyth Teg would be gone and his parents would accuse him of telling tales. Instead, knowing that they did not harm people who were kind to them, he moved closer to see what they were up to.

Creeping closer to the ring he saw that some of the people danced round and round in a perfect circle while others ran about chasing each other. Beautiful women also rode about on small white horses that were finer than any he had seen before. They were all dressed in white and scarlet clothes that shone elegantly, the men wearing red caps and the women in flowing head-dresses that waved about in the gentle winds. It was delightful to see so many happy people merrily dancing about.

Soon enough the fairies noticed the small shepherd boy watching them and beckoned him to enter the circle. The boy was a little nervous at first but he was so enamoured by the glorious spectacle that he couldn't resist drawing closer and closer. Step by step he walked towards them until he placed the tip of one of his shoes within the circle. As soon as it touched the ground his ears were filled with the most uplifting melody that he had ever heard or would ever hear again and, as quickly as he could, he jumped into the circle.

In a moment he was transported to a shining palace that glistened with gold and gems. It was so beautiful and comfortable inside that he wished he could stay there forever. The fairies attended to him throughout the day and gave him whatever he desired. Whereas at home he would eat Tatws Llaeth, or milk and potatoes, they served him with luxurious delicacies that he had never before even dreamed of. He was also served wine in gold goblets by strange invisible forces and by the prettiest of the fairy women.

124

The Tylwyth Teg let him roam anywhere he wanted in the palace and he could also do whatever he wanted. Only one thing was forbidden. There was a fountain in the middle of a luscious garden filled with multi-coloured fish and he was told not to touch this or to drink from its waters. He agreed to leave the fountain and didn't think any more of it for he was very happy in the palace and every day he found something new to occupy himself or some new wonder to marvel at. Soon enough though he tired of the wonders that surrounded him and all he began to think of was the only thing he was not allowed to have.

More and more he thought about the fountain, until one day his curiosity got the better of him. He went to the fountain and plunged his hand straight into the water. As he did so the fish disappeared instantly and when he took his hand out of the water to drink from his palm an almighty shriek resounded throughout the garden. The next moment the whole palace vanished and before he could even blink he was back in the empty field where he had first seen the fairies dancing.

All he could see around him were the same hills and the same sheep that he had always looked at. He shut his eyes and tried to wish himself back into the beautiful palace but, however hard he tried to imagine the scene, when he opened his eyes he had not moved an inch and there was no palace and no fairies to greet him. Although he was very disappointed at first his memories of the palace soon faded and he quickly returned to normal. He was surprised to find that although he imagined he had been in the fairy land for many years he had really only been gone minutes.

This story shows how easy it was for mortals to enter the Otherworld through fairy circles and these circles still litter the countryside, sometimes concentrating in certain well known 'fairy haunts'. The fairies liked nothing better than to dance around them throughout the night and many a person has been tempted by their invitation to join them. They were not fussy who they dragged into their circles either, for an elderly priest from St Dogmaels was once forced to dance with them from night until daybreak. The old man who said this was also from St Dogmaels and he described the whole parish as being awash with fairies who took many people away with them. A local fisherman was said to have been led astray by the fairies on the way home from a wedding and he only found

125

his way home using the North Star. In cases like this however it seems obvious that the fairies were often used as an excuse for drunkenness.

In this story the hardest thing to do was not actually to get to the Otherworld but to stay there. The natural curiosity of mortals often leads to their fall from grace and Celtic tradition is no exception. Many a Welsh Otherworld tale ends with the visitor being cast out after breaking a sacred rule due to human greed, curiosity or just through their ignorance of fairy ways. This type of story always concentrates on the failures of mankind and how humans do not belong with the fairies as they are perfect beings and totally separate from us. The mortality of the guest in the fairy land always becomes apparent and because they do not belong the sanctity of the Otherworld is inevitably broken.

The fountain that the shepherd was told not to touch is directly related to an important symbol found in the world of the Celtic gods. The fountain, bowl or well was the centre of the Otherworld realms and it was the common source of all wisdom and knowledge. It was also dangerous to mortals as shown by how Pryderi and Rhiannon were spirited away after touching the marble fountain in the magical fortress that appeared in Dyfed. Likewise in the Welsh romance of Owain the fountain is found in the middle of the Otherworld below a great tree. Owain is told to take some of its water and throw it on a stone nearby and this induces a terrible hail shower after which the Lord of the Otherworld appears to fight Owain to the death.

In these examples the defilement of the waters of the sacred fountain always caused an adverse reaction to the mortal. This is because the bowl or fountain was the mythological centre and the very heart of the Otherworld, the sacred spring of creation and birth. In the shepherd's story another ancient symbol of the fountain survives as the multi-coloured fish in the fountain. These fish were not just in the tale for novelty value because they are related to the fish who lived in the sacred well of creation. In Irish myth a hazelnut tree grows over the well at the centre of the Otherworld and these nuts of inspiration feed the salmon of knowledge who lives in the sacred well. This salmon is the divine source of poetic inspiration in Celtic culture and the coloured fish at the bottom of the sacred fountain in our story is the folk memory of this divine

126

part of the Otherworld. The symbols of the fairy stories are therefore not just arbitrary creations but are deeply embedded into Celtic myth.

## The Tradegy of Llech y Derwydd

The shepherd boy in the story just told may have lost the Otherworld forever but in comparison with some other fairy stories he had a lucky escape. He had managed to spend years in the fairy world yet only one real day had elapsed but this was the exception to the rule. The fairy lands were not in tune with this world and could cause great sorrow as this story, 'The Heir of Llech y Derwydd' shows. It was collected by the Rev. Benjamin Williams who had a great interest in folklore and was otherwise known by his bardic name of Gwynionydd. The exact position of Llech y Derwydd is unknown but Rev. Williams accepted the tale as taking place in Cemais in North Pembrokeshire. The tale was published originally in Welsh so it has been translated.

There was a boy of Llech y Derwydd who was his parents' only child and therefore the sole inheritor of the farm and its land. Because of this he was very dear to his parents, the light of both his father's and his mother's eyes. The head servant and the son of the house were close companions, as close as two brothers or two best friends. The servant and the boy were so friendly that the woman of the house would always prepare the servant's clothes exactly the same as the boy's. These two lads fell in love with two beautiful women who were highly respected in the region and great was the pleasure at Llech y Derwydd. Soon the two pairs were joined in holy marriage and there was great merriment at the double wedding.

The servant soon had a convenient place to live in the land of Llech y Derwydd and about six months after the son's marriage he and his friend went out hunting. The servant withdrew into some deserted nook and looked for game, soon returning to his companion. But when he got back there was no sign of him anywhere. He continued to look around for a while, shouting and whistling but there was not one trace of his friend. In the end the servant went home to Llech y Derwydd expecting to see him there but nobody had heard anything about him.

The family worried throughout the night and by the next day they

127

were worrying even more. They went to the spot where the servant had last seen his friend and his mother and wife wept, fearing the worst. His father dealt with the worry a little bit better than the man's mother and wife but he too looked like he was half mad. They looked at the place where he had last been and to their great surprise and anxiety they perceived a fairy circle close to the spot. At this spot the servant then remembered that at the time of the disappearance he heard the sound of a very enchanting melody coming from somewhere.

They decided at once that he was unfortunate enough to have wandered into a fairy circle and from there had been transported away to no-one knew where. Weeks and months passed and the wife of the son of Llech y Derwyd had a baby. The young father was not there to see his child and that was very saddening for the old folk. However the little boy grew up into the image of his father and he was very dear in his grandmother's and grandfather's eyes. In truth he was everything to them. He grew up to manhood and married a girl in the neighbourhood. She was pretty enough but there wasn't a word heard about her family being either good or amiable people. Soon the grandparents died and their daughter-in-law, the boy's mother, died also.

On one windy afternoon in October the family of Llech y Derwydd saw a tall, thin old man with his beard and his hair like the snow, and this old man was approaching very slowly towards the house. The servant girls gazed mockingly through the window and the mistress of the house laughed at the old man, lifting up the children one after the other to see him coming. He came to the door and went boldly into the house asking for his parents. The woman replied rudely with unusual satire 'What is the drunken old man doing coming here' she said. They thought that he had been drinking for he surely wouldn't have acted like that normally.

The old man looked surprised and very anxious and he looked at everything in the house with great wonder but the thing he noticed the most was the little children on the floor. He looked full of disappointment and grief. He told the whole story about how he was out hunting yesterday and that he had now returned. The woman said to him that she heard a story about her husband's father that took place in the years before her birth. Some said that he had gotten lost while hunting and never returned but her father had said

128

to her that these tales weren't true and that he had been killed.

The woman soon became wild and totally out of her mind and wanted the old man to go outside. The old man was agitated and said that he was the owner of the house and he should have what was his right. He went outside to see his possessions and soon went to the servant's house. To his surprise things had changed a lot there. After conversing for a while with an elderly man by the fire the one looked at the other more and more intently. The old man told him about the fate of his friend, the son of Llech y Derwydd and they deliberately talked about childhood things. It all seemed like a dream.

Soon the old man by the fire decided that the newcomer in the corner was his old friend, the visitor was the son of Llech y Derwydd who had returned from the fairy lands after half a century. He believed the fate of the old man with the white beard and they talked and questioned each other for many hours.

The old man was told that the present master of Llech y Derwydd, his very own son, was away from home that day. The old visitor was given food to eat but to everyone's great astonishment he fell dead on the spot after eating. The cause of this was that he had eaten food after living in the fairy world for so long. His old friend insisted on seeing him buried beside his family. After this there was always to be a curse on the generations in Llech y Derwydd until the house was sold nine times due to the surliness of the woman to her father in law.

This type of tale is common to all the Celtic countries and it deals with the difference in time between the fairy and the real world. This peculiarity is always turned into a great tragedy by the story teller and what makes this story worse is that there is no evil in the story and no bad characters to hate. The fairies do not purposely take the young mortal and likewise the man has done no bad deeds but the outcome of the chance visit to the Otherworld is truly terrible. The man never sees his unborn child and when he returns after only one day his home is a foreign place peopled by strangers and his beloved wife and family are in their graves. The two worlds are separated for a very good reason and the story gives a very harrowing reason for this.

The fate of the old man's body was the result of returning from the fairy world after being gone so long from the mortal world.

129

When you crossed back into real time your body also returned back to its natural age in a matter of minutes. In the Irish tale of 'The Voyage of Bran' when the heroes return from their voyage to the Otherworld islands they go to the coast of Ireland and Bran introduces himself to some people on the shore. They say they know of him and his journey from their ancient tales and soon one of Bran's companions jumps from the ship onto the beach. The tale says 'as soon as he touched the earth of Ireland, forthwith he was a heap of ashes, as though he had been in the earth for many hundred years.' This tale is over one thousand years old and the same terrible fate appears in our hundred year old story, illustrating how continuous the fairy traditions were.

### Pergrin and the Mermaids

Considering that Pembrokeshire is a peninsula surrounded with water it is hardly surprising to find tales of sea fairies in the area. These were considered to be a variety of the Tylwyth Teg and are also known by the popular name of mermaids. They were much admired by fisherman in the same way that the Knockers, or 'mine fairies' were respected by miners. The mermaids knew all about the sea and its weather and so they were great allies on the dangerous waters if their help could be gained, as the following story shows.

A fisherman named Pergrin was, one fine Autumn day, on his way around the rocks of Pen Cemmes on the Pembrokeshire side of Cardigan Bay. To his surprise in a recess in the rocks he came across a mermaid busily combing her hair. Her usual alertness and caution had been forgotten in her eagerness to look her best for the mermen and so Pergrin was able to get right behind her and capture her in one of his nets. He took the mermaid into his boat and was surprised to hear her speaking fluent Welsh. She was not happy however and wept sorrowfully, her hair soon becoming all tangled in knots. She begged Pergrin to let her go and eventually promised to give him three shouts of warning when he needed them the most if he let her free. At hearing this Pergrin, who never really meant to hurt her, took her out to sea and let her free in her world.

He did not see or hear from her for many weeks after this and he simply got on with his fishing, thinking no more of the affair, other than to marvel at it. But one calm and warm afternoon as he was

130

môr Forwyn

out fishing on his boat the mermaid's head appeared out of the water alongside. 'Pergrin, Pergrin, Pergrin!' she shouted, 'take up your nets, take up your nets, take up your nets!' and then she disappeared back into the water. Without a moment's thought Pergrin and his friend on the boat drew up their nets and hastened for the shore. The moment they reached Pwll Cam on the coast a terrible storm hit the sea with little warning and for the next few hours it raged all around them while they were safely on land. By the next day eighteen men who had gone out with them in their boats were drowned and it was only the mermaid's warning that saved the lives of Pergrin and his friend.

Another encounter with mermaids took place near the bay of Porth y Rhaw north of St Davids. On a quite and calm day when the flowers blossomed and the sun glistened on the rocks only gentle waves lapped against the shore. This beautiful weather enticed one of the children of Rhys Ddwfn to go to the cliffs and sit for a while atop one of the rocks to play with her hair in the sunlight. In a nearby quarry some who were weary of working on the hard stones of the earth decided to travel down to the shore for a rest. They soon spotted the mermaid and as they drew closer they saw that although half her body was the same as any of the beautiful girls of Wales the other half was just the same as the fish of the deep.

They talked to her and although she was surprised at seeing the men they were equally surprised when she spoke back to them in Welsh saying 'Reaping in Pembrokeshire and weeding in Carmarthenshire' before she entered the sea and went on her way home. This mermaid must have been an admirer of Pembrokeshire for this saying is one of those regional jibes that are still used today. It must have referred to the bounty of the land in the first county and the barrenness of the other.

A mermaid is also said to have been caught by some men near Llanwnda. They managed to hold this fairy for longer than the others and kept her securely for some time. Soon enough however she begged to be let free and offered the people some advice. They could not refuse the poor girl's wishes and so when she was released she gave the household three pieces of advice. Unfortunately the tale's reciter only remembered one about how to sweeten a dish known as pottage and so she doesn't seem to have saved their lives in this case. Perhaps in older times this tale was longer and the mermaid granted her captors three wishes as was the case when a Scottish mermaid was caught in North Harris.

## Ianto and the Fairy Money

The tales of the Tylwyth Teg were not just about mythical lands, fountains and mermaids. They were folktales and because of this the Tylwyth Teg appear frequently in the normal lives of the folk who told the tales. Just as the humans visited the Otherworld so the fairies also often visited our world, living secretly around the houses and hedgerows of the countryside. The Tylwyth Teg were especially fond of tidiness and many maids and housewives knew the importance they attached to a clean house. The fairies also appreciated kindness and would often reward a bath and a jug of milk left out for them on a cold night. It was always wise to try and please the fairies in this way for it could mean riches and the end of financial worry.

Ianto Llewellyn was one of these kind people, he lived in Llanfihangel parish and would often leave the fire burning throughout the night to keep the Tylwyth Teg warm. He knew they came to his house for he could hear them in his kitchen. One night as he lay in bed wide awake he heard the fairies come along as usual. One of them said 'It is a cold night and I wish we could have some cheese and bread but this poor man only has a morsel left, plenty enough for us but he might starve without it!' Ianto cried back in reply 'Take anything you want, you are welcome!' and then turned over to sleep.

The next morning he went to his kitchen to see if the fairies had left any scraps for him. He opened the cupboard door and cried out 'O'r anwyl! what's this!' and there in the cupboard was a large block of fine cheese and two fresh loaves of bread. Ianto turned to the forest where he knew the fairies lived and cried 'Lwc dda i ti!' which means 'good luck to you' and he also wished that they would never go hungry or poor. As soon as he said this he looked across to the hob and saw, to his amazement, a shilling resting there.

Every morning from that day onwards he would wake up and find another shilling on the hob, and now he did not want for bread or cheese for he had them, as well as tobacco and beer, in abundance.

He soon became known in the parish as 'Lucky Ianto' for he was a rich man although he never did any work. He even had enough to keep a wife in a little luxury and he would have had riches for the rest of his life if it was not for the inquisitiveness of Betsi, his wife. She wanted to know where the money was coming from for she did not want any secrets between them. 'Shame on you,' she said to Ianto who replied, 'but if I tell you we will have no more money!' 'So!' said Betsi, who knew of the fairies' habits, 'it is fairy money then.' Ianto cursed under his breath and sulked out of the house admitting that it was the fairies. He thrust his hands into his pockets and where there had been seven shillings previously now there were only worthless pieces of paper and from then on no more money appeared in his house for the fairies' secret had been discovered.

The Tylwyth Teg appreciated secrecy as well as honesty and the few brief legends I have given about them here only represents the smallest tip of what was once told around many a fire in Pembrokeshire. Fairy lore is important in giving us glimpses of the ancient customs and beliefs of Welsh culture and they are not merely quaint tales for children. Places in Pembrokeshire like Bwci Dwll, the Bwci or 'Fairy Hollow', reminds us how fairy feet once graced the green grass of the county. This Otherworld of the ever young, which is in all of our minds as a spirit of freedom, lies just out of our view somewhere off the coast of Pembrokeshire.

# Further Reading

In this book I have tried to give a wide and varied account of the variety, antiquity and beauty of the legends and folk tales that are known about Pembrokeshire.  I hope that they will show that the landscape has its own history and that there are interesting traditions and legends to be found all around the country.  I have not exhausted all the legends and tales and there is a wide variety of books that give further information about the subject.  The short list that follows is therefore designed to give the reader more avenues to explore if they wish to read more about the legends in this book.

It is very rewarding to read the Mabinogion stories in their original and complete forms and the translations never fail to amaze and intrigue.  As well as the stories of Pwyll, Pryderi and Manawydan the story of the Twrch Trwyth and three Arthurian romances are also included in the Mabinogion.  The three folklore books are also full of wonderful stories that were told to the authors first hand by the people of Wales.  The book on the lives of the British saints is a good introduction to the period and includes the lives of Dewi, Teilo and Canna as well as many other famous Welsh saints.  If you are living in or just visiting Wales you will surely find stories in these books to help colour your local area.

Jeffrey Gantz (trans), The Mabinogion. Penguin Books. 1976.

Gwyn and Thomas Jones, The Mabinogion, J.M.Dent. 1949.

Jonathon Caredig Davies, Folklore of West and Mid Wales, 1911. Reprinted by Llanerch Press. 1992.

John Rhys, Celtic Folk Lore: Welsh and Manx, 2 Vols. 1983. Reprinted by Wildwood House, 1980.

W. Howells, Cambrian Superstitions, 1831. Llanerch reprint. 1991.

Derek Bryce, ed. Lives of the British Saints, S. Baring Gould & John Fisher,  selected reprint from the original four-volume work, Llanerch. 1990.

# Bibliography

Bager, A, and Green, F. *The Chapel Traditionally Attributed to St Patrick, Whitesand Bay, Pembrokeshire*, Archaelogia Cambrensis Vol 5 (1924), pp.87-120.

Baring-Gould, S. and John Fisher, *Lives of the British Saints*, 4 Vols. London.

Bartrum, Peter C, ed. *Early Welsh Genealogical Tracts*, Cardiff: University of Wales Press. 1966.

Bowen, E.G., *Saints, Seaways and Settlements in the Celtic Lands*, Cardiff: University of Wales Press. 1977.

Bromwich, Rachel, *Pedwar Marchog Ar Hugain Llys Arthur*, Transactions of the Honourable Society of Cymmrodorion (1957), pp.116-132.

Bromwich, Rachel, ed. *Trioedd Ynys Prydein*, Cardiff: University of Wales Press. 1962.

Bromwich, Rachel, ed. *The Beginnings of Welsh Poetry: Studies by Sir Ifor Williams*, Cardiff: University of Wales Press. 1972.

Bromwich, Rachel, *The Mabinogion and Lady Charlotte Guest*, Transactions of the Honourable Society of Cymmrodorion (1986), pp.127-141.

Chadwick, Nora Kershaw, *Intellectual Life in West Wales in the Last Days of the Celtic Church*, Studies in the Early British Church, ed. Nora K. Chadwick, Cambridge: University Press, 1958, pp.121-182.

Chadwick, Owen, *The Evidence of Dedications in the Early History of the Welsh Church*, Studies in Early British History, ed. Nora K. Chadwick, Cambridge: University Press. 1954. pp.173-188.

Charles, B.G., *The Place names of Pembrokeshire*, 2Vols. Aberystwyth: National Library of Wales. 1992.

Clancy, Joseph, *The Earliest Welsh Poetry*, London: Macmillan. 1970.

Coileain, S.O., *A Thematic Study of the Tale Pwyll Pendeuic Dyuet*, Studia Celtica 12/13 (1978), pp.78-82.

Coleman, S.J., *Lore and Legend of Pembrokeshire*, Treasury of Folklore No 26. Mimeo. 1954.

Coplestone-Crow, Bruce, 'The Dual Nature of the Irish Colonization of Dyfed in the Dark Ages*, Studia Celtica 16/17 (1981), pp.1-24.

Cross, T. and C. Slover, eds. *Ancient Irish Tales*, New York: Barnes and Noble. 1996.

Davies, J.C., *Folk-Lore of West and Mid Wales*, Aberystwyth. 1911.

Dickins, Bruce, *Dewi Sant in Early English Kalendars and Place-Names, Celt & Saxon*, ed. Nora Chadwick, Cambridge: University Press. 1963. pp.206-209.

Doble, G.H., *Lives of the Welsh Saints*, Cardiff: University of Wales Press.

Evans-Wentz, W.Y., *The Fairy Faith in Celtic Countries*, Oxford: Oxford University Press. 1911.

Ford, Patrick, *Prolegomena to a Reading of the Mabinogi: Pwyll and Manawydan*, Studia Celtica 16/17 (1981), pp.110-125.

Gantz, Jeffrey (Trans), *The Mabinogion*, London: Penguin. 1976.

Gerald of Wales, *Expugnatio Hibernica: The Conquest of Ireland*, Eds A.B. Scott, F.X. Martin. Dublin: Royal Irish Academy. 1978.

Gerald of Wales, *The Journey through Wales & The Description of Wales.*, trans. Thorpe, Lewis, Penguin Books. 1974.

Graham Jones, J., *Hanes Cymru*, Caerdydd: Gwasg Prifysgol Cymru. 1994.

Grooms, C.R., *Giants in Welsh Folklore and Tradition*, PhD Thesis University of Wales Aberystwyth. 1988.

Gruffydd, *Geraint, and Huw Parri Owen, 'The Earliest Mention of St David?'*, Bulletin of the Board of Celtic Studies XVII (1958), pp.185-193.

Hanson-Smith, Elizabeth, *Pwyll Prince of Dyfed*, Studia Celtica 16/17 (1981), pp.126-134.

Harries, D.C., *Caldey Monastery Isle, Narbeth Tenby & Whitland:* H.G. Walters. Undated.

Howells, R., *Caldey*, Llandysul: Gomer. 1984.

Howells, W., *Cambrian Superstitions*, 1831. Reprint Felinfach: Llanerch. 1991.

James, J.A., ed. and transl. *Rhigyfarch's Life of St David*, Cardiff: University of Wales Press. 1967.

Jones, Francis, *The Holy Wells of Wales*, Cardiff: University of Wales Press. 1954.

Jones, Francis, *Llanrheithan*, The Pembrokeshire Historian No 3 (1971), pp.53-80.

Jones, Thomas, *The Black Book of Carmarthen Stanzas of the Graves*, Proceedings of the British Academy 53 (1967), pp.97-137.

Koch, John T., *A Welsh Window on the Iron Age: Manawydan, Mandubracios*, Cambridge Medieval Celtic Studies 14 (1987), pp17-52.

McKenna, Catherine, *The Theme of Sovereignty in Pwyll'*, Bulletin of the Board of Celtic Studies XXIX (1982), pp.35-52.

Meurig-Evans, H., *The Modern Welsh Dictionary: Y Geiriadur Cyfoes*, Abertawe: Christopher Davies. 1982.

Meyer, Kuno, *The Voyage of Bran*, 1895 Reprinted Felinfach: Llanerch 1995

Morris, J., ed & trans., *Nennius: British History and The Welsh Annals*, London: Phillimore. 1980.

Morris, Lewis, *Celtic Remains*, Ed. Silvan Evans. London: Honourable Society of Cymmrodorion. 1878.

Nash-Williams, V.E., *The Early Christian Monuments of Wales*, Cardiff: University of Wales Press. 1950.

North, F.J., *Sunken Cities*, Cardiff: University of Wales Press. 1954.

Rees, Sian, *A Guide to Ancient & Historical Wales: Dyfed*, London: HMSO. 1992.

Rhys, J., et al., *Pembrokeshire Antiquities*, Solva: H.W. Williams. 1897.

Rhys, John, *Celtic Folklore Welsh & Manx*, 2Vols. Oxford: Oxford University Press. 1901.

Ross, Anne, *Pagan Celtic Britain*, London: Routledge Keegan & Paul Ltd. 1967.

Sikes, Wirt, *British Goblins*, London: Sampson Law. 1880.

Williams, Ifor. *The Beginnings of Welsh Poetry - studies by Ifor Williams*, Cardiff, University of Wales Press, 1980.

Williams, Mary, *More About Bleddri*, Etudes Celtica, Vol II.

Wood, Juliette, *The Calumniated Wife in Medieval Welsh Literature*, Cambridge Medieval Celtic Studies 10 (1985), pp.25-38.